50 American Restaurant Dessert Recipes for Home

By: Kelly Johnson

Table of Contents

- Classic Cheeseburger
- Fried Chicken Sandwich
- BBQ Pulled Pork Sandwich
- Reuben Sandwich
- Buffalo Chicken Wrap
- Grilled Cheese and Tomato Soup
- Club Sandwich
- Philly Cheesesteak
- Fish Tacos
- Cobb Salad
- Caesar Salad with Grilled Chicken
- Turkey and Avocado Sandwich
- Meatball Sub
- BLT Sandwich
- Chicken Caesar Wrap
- Sloppy Joes
- BBQ Chicken Pizza
- Spinach and Artichoke Dip with Chips
- Chicken Quesadilla
- Buffalo Chicken Salad
- Grilled Portobello Mushroom Burger
- Lobster Roll
- Black Bean Burger
- Chicken Fried Rice
- Macaroni and Cheese
- Beef Chili
- Nachos
- Cornbread and Chili
- Sweet and Sour Chicken
- Philly Cheesesteak Pizza
- Crab Cakes
- Chicken and Waffles

- Tex-Mex Enchiladas
- Shrimp Po' Boy
- Sausage and Peppers Sandwich
- Jambalaya
- Monte Cristo Sandwich
- Greek Salad with Lamb
- BBQ Brisket Sandwich
- Turkey Chili
- Breakfast Burrito
- Cajun Chicken Pasta
- Grilled Veggie Panini
- Pulled Pork Tacos
- Steak Frites
- Chicken Parmesan Sandwich
- Beef Stroganoff
- Sweet Potato Fries
- Loaded Potato Skins
- Teriyaki Chicken Bowl

Classic Cheeseburger

Ingredients:

- **Ground Beef:** 1 lb (80% lean, 20% fat)
- **Salt:** 1 tsp
- **Black Pepper:** 1/2 tsp
- **Cheddar Cheese:** 4 slices
- **Burger Buns:** 4 (preferably sesame or brioche)
- **Lettuce:** 4 leaves
- **Tomato:** 1 large, sliced
- **Pickles:** 8 slices
- **Red Onion:** 1 small, sliced
- **Mayonnaise:** 4 tbsp
- **Ketchup:** 4 tbsp
- **Mustard:** 4 tsp
- **Butter:** 2 tbsp (for toasting buns)

Instructions:

1. **Preheat the Grill or Skillet:**
    - Heat your grill to high or your skillet over medium-high heat.
2. **Form the Patties:**
    - Divide the ground beef into 4 equal portions. Gently shape each portion into a patty about 3/4-inch thick. Make a small indent in the center of each patty with your thumb (this helps prevent bulging in the center as they cook).
3. **Season the Patties:**
    - Season both sides of each patty with salt and black pepper.
4. **Cook the Patties:**
    - Place the patties on the grill or skillet. Cook for about 4 minutes on each side for medium-rare, or until the desired doneness is reached. About 1 minute before the burgers are done, place a slice of cheddar cheese on each patty and cover with a lid to melt.
5. **Toast the Buns:**
    - While the burgers are cooking, spread butter on the cut sides of the burger buns. Toast them on a separate skillet or grill until golden brown.
6. **Assemble the Burgers:**
    - Spread mayonnaise, ketchup, and mustard on the bottom half of each bun.
    - Place a leaf of lettuce on top of the condiments.
    - Add the cooked cheeseburger patty on top of the lettuce.
    - Layer on tomato slices, pickles, and red onion slices.
    - Top with the other half of the bun.
7. **Serve:**

- Serve the cheeseburgers immediately with your favorite side dishes, like fries or a salad.

Enjoy your delicious classic cheeseburger!

Fried Chicken Sandwich

Ingredients:

- **Chicken Breasts:** 4 boneless, skinless
- **Buttermilk:** 2 cups
- **All-Purpose Flour:** 1 cup
- **Cornstarch:** 1/2 cup
- **Paprika:** 1 tbsp
- **Garlic Powder:** 1 tbsp
- **Onion Powder:** 1 tbsp
- **Cayenne Pepper:** 1 tsp
- **Salt:** 1 tsp
- **Black Pepper:** 1/2 tsp
- **Baking Powder:** 1 tsp
- **Eggs:** 2, beaten
- **Vegetable Oil:** For frying
- **Burger Buns:** 4
- **Mayonnaise:** 1/2 cup
- **Lettuce:** 4 leaves
- **Pickles:** 8 slices
- **Hot Sauce:** Optional, to taste

Instructions:

1. **Prepare the Chicken:**
   - Pound the chicken breasts to an even thickness (about 1/2 inch thick) for even cooking.
2. **Marinate the Chicken:**
   - Place the chicken breasts in a bowl and cover with buttermilk. Marinate in the refrigerator for at least 1 hour, or overnight for best results.
3. **Prepare the Breading:**
   - In a large bowl, combine the flour, cornstarch, paprika, garlic powder, onion powder, cayenne pepper, salt, black pepper, and baking powder.
4. **Bread the Chicken:**
   - Remove the chicken from the buttermilk, allowing excess to drip off. Dredge each piece of chicken in the seasoned flour mixture, pressing to adhere. Dip the chicken back into the beaten eggs, then dredge again in the flour mixture for an extra crispy coating.
5. **Heat the Oil:**
   - Heat about 1-2 inches of vegetable oil in a large skillet over medium-high heat to 350°F (175°C). Use a thermometer to check the temperature.
6. **Fry the Chicken:**

- Carefully place the breaded chicken into the hot oil. Fry in batches, being careful not to overcrowd the pan. Cook for about 5-7 minutes per side, or until golden brown and cooked through (internal temperature should reach 165°F or 74°C). Drain on paper towels.

7. **Toast the Buns:**
    - While the chicken is frying, toast the burger buns in a skillet or under the broiler until golden brown.
8. **Assemble the Sandwich:**
    - Spread mayonnaise on the bottom half of each bun. Add a leaf of lettuce, followed by a fried chicken breast. Top with pickles and, if desired, a dash of hot sauce. Place the top half of the bun on the sandwich.
9. **Serve:**
    - Serve the fried chicken sandwiches hot with your favorite side dishes, such as coleslaw or French fries.

Enjoy your delicious homemade Fried Chicken Sandwich!

BBQ Pulled Pork Sandwich

Ingredients:

- **Pork Shoulder (Boston Butt):** 4-5 lbs
- **BBQ Rub:**
    - **Brown Sugar:** 1/4 cup
    - **Paprika:** 2 tbsp
    - **Salt:** 1 tbsp
    - **Black Pepper:** 1 tbsp
    - **Garlic Powder:** 1 tbsp
    - **Onion Powder:** 1 tbsp
    - **Cayenne Pepper:** 1/2 tsp (optional, for heat)
- **BBQ Sauce:** 2 cups (your favorite brand or homemade)
- **Apple Cider Vinegar:** 1/4 cup
- **Chicken Broth:** 1 cup
- **Burger Buns:** 4-6
- **Coleslaw:** Optional, for topping
- **Pickles:** Optional, for topping

Instructions:

1. **Prepare the Pork Shoulder:**
    - Pat the pork shoulder dry with paper towels. Combine all the BBQ rub ingredients in a bowl and rub the mixture all over the pork shoulder. Let it sit for at least 1 hour, or overnight in the refrigerator for more flavor.
2. **Cook the Pork:**
    - **Slow Cooker Method:**
        - Place the seasoned pork shoulder in the slow cooker. Pour the apple cider vinegar and chicken broth around the pork.
        - Cover and cook on low for 8-10 hours or until the pork is very tender and easily shreds with a fork.
    - **Oven Method:**
        - Preheat your oven to 300°F (150°C). Place the pork shoulder in a roasting pan and cover tightly with aluminum foil.
        - Roast for 4-5 hours, or until the pork is very tender. You may need to add a little more liquid (broth) during cooking if it evaporates.
3. **Shred the Pork:**
    - Once the pork is cooked, remove it from the slow cooker or oven and transfer it to a large bowl. Use two forks to shred the pork into bite-sized pieces.
4. **Mix with BBQ Sauce:**
    - Discard any large pieces of fat from the cooking liquid. Mix the shredded pork with the BBQ sauce and a bit of the cooking liquid (if using a slow cooker) or a bit

of additional chicken broth for moisture. Stir until well combined and heated through.
5. **Prepare the Buns:**
   - Toast the burger buns in a skillet or under the broiler until golden brown.
6. **Assemble the Sandwiches:**
   - Spoon a generous portion of the BBQ pulled pork onto the bottom half of each bun. Top with coleslaw and pickles if desired. Place the top half of the bun on the sandwich.
7. **Serve:**
   - Serve the BBQ pulled pork sandwiches hot with extra BBQ sauce on the side and your favorite side dishes, such as baked beans or fries.

Enjoy your flavorful and tender BBQ Pulled Pork Sandwiches!

Reuben Sandwich

Ingredients:

- **Pork Shoulder (Boston Butt):** 4-5 lbs
- **BBQ Rub:**
    - **Brown Sugar:** 1/4 cup
    - **Paprika:** 2 tbsp
    - **Salt:** 1 tbsp
    - **Black Pepper:** 1 tbsp
    - **Garlic Powder:** 1 tbsp
    - **Onion Powder:** 1 tbsp
    - **Cayenne Pepper:** 1/2 tsp (optional, for heat)
- **BBQ Sauce:** 2 cups (your favorite brand or homemade)
- **Apple Cider Vinegar:** 1/4 cup
- **Chicken Broth:** 1 cup
- **Burger Buns:** 4-6
- **Coleslaw:** Optional, for topping
- **Pickles:** Optional, for topping

Instructions:

1. **Prepare the Pork Shoulder:**
    - Pat the pork shoulder dry with paper towels. Combine all the BBQ rub ingredients in a bowl and rub the mixture all over the pork shoulder. Let it sit for at least 1 hour, or overnight in the refrigerator for more flavor.
2. **Cook the Pork:**
    - **Slow Cooker Method:**
        - Place the seasoned pork shoulder in the slow cooker. Pour the apple cider vinegar and chicken broth around the pork.
        - Cover and cook on low for 8-10 hours or until the pork is very tender and easily shreds with a fork.
    - **Oven Method:**
        - Preheat your oven to 300°F (150°C). Place the pork shoulder in a roasting pan and cover tightly with aluminum foil.
        - Roast for 4-5 hours, or until the pork is very tender. You may need to add a little more liquid (broth) during cooking if it evaporates.
3. **Shred the Pork:**
    - Once the pork is cooked, remove it from the slow cooker or oven and transfer it to a large bowl. Use two forks to shred the pork into bite-sized pieces.
4. **Mix with BBQ Sauce:**
    - Discard any large pieces of fat from the cooking liquid. Mix the shredded pork with the BBQ sauce and a bit of the cooking liquid (if using a slow cooker) or a bit

of additional chicken broth for moisture. Stir until well combined and heated through.
5. **Prepare the Buns:**
    - Toast the burger buns in a skillet or under the broiler until golden brown.
6. **Assemble the Sandwiches:**
    - Spoon a generous portion of the BBQ pulled pork onto the bottom half of each bun. Top with coleslaw and pickles if desired. Place the top half of the bun on the sandwich.
7. **Serve:**
    - Serve the BBQ pulled pork sandwiches hot with extra BBQ sauce on the side and your favorite side dishes, such as baked beans or fries.

Enjoy your flavorful and tender BBQ Pulled Pork Sandwiches!

Buffalo Chicken Wrap

Ingredients:

- **Chicken Breasts:** 2, boneless and skinless
- **Buffalo Sauce:** 1/2 cup (store-bought or homemade)
- **All-Purpose Flour:** 1/2 cup
- **Eggs:** 2, beaten
- **Breadcrumbs:** 1 cup (plain or seasoned)
- **Vegetable Oil:** For frying
- **Large Flour Tortillas:** 4
- **Romaine Lettuce:** 2 cups, shredded
- **Ranch Dressing or Blue Cheese Dressing:** 1/2 cup
- **Shredded Carrots:** 1/2 cup
- **Celery Sticks:** 1/2 cup, chopped
- **Cheddar Cheese:** 1/2 cup, shredded (optional)

Instructions:

1. **Prepare the Chicken:**
    - Pound the chicken breasts to an even thickness (about 1/2 inch) for even cooking.
2. **Bread the Chicken:**
    - Set up a breading station with three shallow bowls: one with flour, one with beaten eggs, and one with breadcrumbs.
    - Dredge each chicken breast in the flour, shaking off excess. Dip in the beaten eggs, then coat with breadcrumbs, pressing to adhere.
3. **Fry the Chicken:**
    - Heat about 1/4 inch of vegetable oil in a large skillet over medium heat.
    - Fry the chicken breasts for about 4-5 minutes per side, or until golden brown and cooked through (internal temperature should reach 165°F or 74°C). Drain on paper towels.
4. **Coat the Chicken with Buffalo Sauce:**
    - Once the chicken is cooked, slice it into strips. Toss the chicken strips in a bowl with the buffalo sauce until well coated.
5. **Prepare the Wraps:**
    - Warm the flour tortillas in a skillet or microwave until pliable.
    - Spread a layer of ranch or blue cheese dressing on each tortilla.
    - Add a handful of shredded lettuce, shredded carrots, and chopped celery.
    - Place a generous amount of buffalo chicken strips on top. Add shredded cheddar cheese if using.
6. **Wrap It Up:**

- Fold in the sides of the tortilla, then roll it up tightly from the bottom to enclose the filling.
7. **Serve:**
    - Slice the wraps in half diagonally if desired. Serve with extra ranch or blue cheese dressing for dipping and enjoy!

This Buffalo Chicken Wrap is perfect for a quick lunch or a delicious snack!

Grilled Cheese and Tomato Soup

Ingredients:

- **Olive Oil:** 2 tbsp
- **Onion:** 1 medium, chopped
- **Garlic:** 2 cloves, minced
- **Carrots:** 2 medium, peeled and diced
- **Canned Tomatoes:** 2 (14.5 oz) cans, diced or whole (crushed if whole)
- **Vegetable or Chicken Broth:** 2 cups
- **Tomato Paste:** 2 tbsp
- **Sugar:** 1 tsp (optional, to balance acidity)
- **Dried Basil:** 1 tsp (or 2 tsp fresh basil, chopped)
- **Salt and Pepper:** To taste
- **Heavy Cream:** 1/2 cup (optional, for creamier soup)
- **Fresh Basil:** For garnish (optional)

Instructions:

1. **Sauté Vegetables:**
   - Heat olive oil in a large pot over medium heat. Add chopped onion and cook until translucent, about 5 minutes. Add garlic and cook for an additional 1 minute.
2. **Add Carrots:**
   - Add diced carrots and cook for another 5 minutes.
3. **Add Tomatoes and Broth:**
   - Stir in the canned tomatoes, tomato paste, and vegetable or chicken broth. Add sugar if using, dried basil, salt, and pepper. Bring to a boil.
4. **Simmer:**
   - Reduce heat and simmer for 20-25 minutes, until carrots are tender.
5. **Blend the Soup:**
   - Use an immersion blender to puree the soup directly in the pot until smooth. Alternatively, carefully transfer the soup in batches to a blender and puree.
6. **Add Cream (Optional):**
   - Stir in heavy cream if using. Heat the soup gently until warmed through. Adjust seasoning as needed.
7. **Serve:**
   - Ladle the soup into bowls, garnish with fresh basil if desired, and serve with the grilled cheese sandwiches.

Enjoy this classic and comforting combination of grilled cheese and tomato soup!

Club Sandwich

Ingredients:

- **Bread:** 3 slices per sandwich (white, whole wheat, or toasted)
- **Turkey Breast:** 4 oz, cooked and sliced (or use chicken)
- **Ham:** 4 oz, cooked and sliced
- **Bacon:** 4 strips, cooked and crispy
- **Lettuce:** 2-3 leaves
- **Tomato:** 1, sliced
- **Mayonnaise:** 3 tbsp
- **Mustard:** 1 tbsp (optional)
- **Salt and Pepper:** To taste
- **Pickles:** Optional, for garnish

Instructions:

1. **Toast the Bread:**
   - Toast the bread slices until golden brown. You'll need 3 slices per sandwich.
2. **Prepare the Ingredients:**
   - Cook the bacon until crispy and drain on paper towels.
   - Slice the tomato and prepare the lettuce leaves.
3. **Assemble the Sandwich:**
   - **Layer 1:** Spread mayonnaise (and mustard, if using) on one side of a slice of toasted bread. Place it mayo side up on a plate. Layer on the turkey, lettuce, and tomato slices. Season with salt and pepper.
   - **Layer 2:** Top with a second slice of toasted bread. Spread mayonnaise on the top side of this bread. Layer on the ham and bacon.
   - **Layer 3:** Place the final slice of toasted bread on top, mayonnaise side down.
4. **Cut and Serve:**
   - Cut the sandwich diagonally into quarters. Secure each quarter with a toothpick if desired. Garnish with pickles or additional vegetables if you like.
5. **Optional:**
   - Serve with a side of chips, fries, or a small salad.

Enjoy your classic Club Sandwich, perfect for lunch or a hearty snack!

Philly Cheesesteak

Ingredients:

- **Ribeye Steak:** 1 lb, thinly sliced
- **Onions:** 1 large, sliced
- **Bell Peppers:** 1 green and 1 red, sliced (optional)
- **Mushrooms:** 1 cup, sliced (optional)
- **Provolone Cheese:** 4 slices (or use American cheese for a more traditional choice)
- **Hoagie Rolls:** 4, sliced lengthwise
- **Olive Oil:** 2 tbsp
- **Salt and Pepper:** To taste
- **Garlic Powder:** 1/2 tsp (optional)
- **Worcestershire Sauce:** 1 tbsp (optional)

Instructions:

1. **Prepare the Steak:**
   - If the ribeye steak is not pre-sliced, freeze it for about 30 minutes to make it easier to slice thinly. Slice the steak against the grain into thin strips.
2. **Cook the Vegetables:**
   - Heat 1 tablespoon of olive oil in a large skillet over medium heat. Add the sliced onions, bell peppers (if using), and mushrooms (if using). Cook until the vegetables are softened and caramelized, about 8-10 minutes. Season with salt and pepper. Remove from the skillet and set aside.
3. **Cook the Steak:**
   - Add the remaining tablespoon of olive oil to the skillet. Increase the heat to medium-high.
   - Add the sliced steak to the skillet. Cook, stirring frequently, until the steak is browned and cooked through, about 4-5 minutes. Season with salt, pepper, and garlic powder. If using, stir in Worcestershire sauce for extra flavor.
4. **Combine Steak and Vegetables:**
   - Return the cooked vegetables to the skillet with the steak. Stir to combine and heat through.
5. **Add Cheese:**
   - Divide the steak and vegetable mixture into four portions in the skillet. Lay a slice of provolone cheese over each portion. Cover the skillet with a lid for about 1-2 minutes, or until the cheese is melted.
6. **Prepare the Rolls:**
   - While the cheese is melting, split the hoagie rolls and toast them lightly if desired.
7. **Assemble the Sandwiches:**
   - Using a spatula, scoop the cheesy steak and vegetable mixture onto the hoagie rolls.

8. **Serve:**
    - Serve the Philly cheesesteaks hot, with optional condiments like hot peppers or extra cheese if desired.

Enjoy your authentic Philly Cheesesteak!

Fish Tacos

Ingredients:

For the Fish:

- **White Fish Fillets:** 1 lb (such as cod, tilapia, or halibut)
- **Flour:** 1/2 cup
- **Cornmeal:** 1/2 cup
- **Paprika:** 1 tsp
- **Garlic Powder:** 1/2 tsp
- **Onion Powder:** 1/2 tsp
- **Cayenne Pepper:** 1/4 tsp (optional, for heat)
- **Salt:** 1/2 tsp
- **Black Pepper:** 1/4 tsp
- **Egg:** 1, beaten
- **Vegetable Oil:** For frying

For the Slaw:

- **Shredded Cabbage:** 2 cups
- **Shredded Carrots:** 1/2 cup
- **Green Onions:** 2, chopped
- **Cilantro:** 1/4 cup, chopped
- **Lime Juice:** 2 tbsp
- **Mayonnaise:** 1/4 cup
- **Apple Cider Vinegar:** 1 tbsp
- **Salt and Pepper:** To taste

For Serving:

- **Corn or Flour Tortillas:** 8, warmed
- **Lime Wedges:** For garnish
- **Hot Sauce:** Optional
- **Avocado:** Sliced (optional)
- **Fresh Cilantro:** For garnish

Instructions:

1. **Prepare the Slaw:**
   - In a large bowl, combine shredded cabbage, shredded carrots, chopped green onions, and cilantro.
   - In a small bowl, mix lime juice, mayonnaise, and apple cider vinegar. Season with salt and pepper.

- Pour the dressing over the cabbage mixture and toss until well combined. Refrigerate while preparing the fish.

2. **Prepare the Fish:**
    - Cut the fish fillets into bite-sized strips.
    - In a shallow bowl, combine flour, cornmeal, paprika, garlic powder, onion powder, cayenne pepper (if using), salt, and black pepper.
    - Dip each piece of fish into the beaten egg, then dredge in the flour mixture, coating well.
3. **Fry the Fish:**
    - Heat about 1/2 inch of vegetable oil in a large skillet over medium-high heat.
    - Fry the fish pieces in batches, turning occasionally, until golden brown and cooked through, about 3-4 minutes per side. Drain on paper towels.
4. **Assemble the Tacos:**
    - Warm the tortillas in a skillet or microwave.
    - Place a few pieces of fried fish in each tortilla.
    - Top with a generous amount of slaw.
    - Garnish with avocado slices (if using), fresh cilantro, and a squeeze of lime juice.
    - Add hot sauce if desired.
5. **Serve:**
    - Serve the fish tacos immediately with additional lime wedges and your favorite sides.

Enjoy your fresh and flavorful Fish Tacos!

Cobb Salad

Ingredients:

- **Chicken Breasts:** 2 boneless, skinless
- **Olive Oil:** 2 tbsp
- **Salt and Pepper:** To taste
- **Romaine Lettuce:** 6 cups, chopped
- **Tomatoes:** 2 large, diced
- **Avocado:** 1, diced
- **Hard-Boiled Eggs:** 4, peeled and chopped
- **Bacon:** 6 strips, cooked and crumbled
- **Blue Cheese:** 1/2 cup, crumbled
- **Chives:** 2 tbsp, chopped (optional)

For the Dressing:

- **Ranch Dressing or Blue Cheese Dressing:** 1 cup (store-bought or homemade)
- **Red Wine Vinegar:** 1 tbsp (optional, for extra tang)

Instructions:

1. **Cook the Chicken:**
    - Preheat your grill or skillet over medium-high heat.
    - Brush the chicken breasts with olive oil and season with salt and pepper.
    - Grill or cook in the skillet for about 6-8 minutes per side, or until the chicken is cooked through (internal temperature should reach 165°F or 74°C). Let the chicken rest for a few minutes before slicing or chopping into bite-sized pieces.
2. **Prepare the Salad Ingredients:**
    - While the chicken is cooking, prepare the other salad ingredients.
    - Wash and chop the romaine lettuce. Dice the tomatoes and avocado. Peel and chop the hard-boiled eggs. Cook the bacon until crispy and crumble it.
3. **Assemble the Salad:**
    - In a large salad bowl or platter, arrange the chopped romaine lettuce as the base.
    - Arrange rows or sections of diced tomatoes, avocado, chopped hard-boiled eggs, crumbled bacon, and diced chicken on top of the lettuce.
    - Sprinkle the crumbled blue cheese and chopped chives (if using

) over the top.

4. **Prepare the Dressing:**
    - If desired, mix the ranch or blue cheese dressing with red wine vinegar for added tang.
5. **Serve:**

    - Serve the Cobb Salad with the dressing on the side or drizzled over the top.

Enjoy your hearty and flavorful Cobb Salad!

Caesar Salad with Grilled Chicken

Ingredients:

For the Salad:

- **Romaine Lettuce:** 4 cups, chopped
- **Grilled Chicken Breasts:** 2, boneless and skinless, sliced or chopped
- **Croutons:** 1 cup (store-bought or homemade)
- **Parmesan Cheese:** 1/2 cup, shaved or grated

For the Caesar Dressing:

- **Mayonnaise:** 1/2 cup
- **Parmesan Cheese:** 1/4 cup, grated
- **Garlic:** 2 cloves, minced
- **Lemon Juice:** 2 tbsp
- **Anchovy Paste:** 1 tbsp (optional, for authentic flavor)
- **Dijon Mustard:** 1 tsp
- **Worcestershire Sauce:** 1 tsp
- **Salt:** 1/4 tsp
- **Black Pepper:** 1/4 tsp
- **Olive Oil:** 2 tbsp

Instructions:

1. **Prepare the Chicken:**
   - Preheat your grill or skillet over medium-high heat.
   - Season the chicken breasts with salt and pepper, and brush with a little olive oil.
   - Grill or cook the chicken for 6-8 minutes per side, or until the internal temperature reaches 165°F (74°C) and the juices run clear. Let the chicken rest for a few minutes before slicing or chopping into bite-sized pieces.
2. **Make the Caesar Dressing:**
   - In a medium bowl, whisk together mayonnaise, Parmesan cheese, minced garlic, lemon juice, anchovy paste (if using), Dijon mustard, Worcestershire sauce, salt, pepper, and olive oil until smooth and well combined.
3. **Assemble the Salad:**
   - In a large bowl, toss the chopped romaine lettuce with the Caesar dressing until evenly coated.
   - Add the grilled chicken pieces on top of the dressed lettuce.
   - Sprinkle croutons and shaved Parmesan cheese over the salad.
4. **Serve:**
   - Serve the Caesar Salad with Grilled Chicken immediately, with extra Parmesan cheese and croutons on the side if desired.

Enjoy your classic and delicious Caesar Salad with Grilled Chicken!

Turkey and Avocado Sandwich

Ingredients:

- **Sliced Turkey Breast:** 8 oz (deli-style or cooked)
- **Avocado:** 1, sliced
- **Whole Wheat or Multigrain Bread:** 4 slices (or your preferred bread)
- **Lettuce:** 4 leaves (romaine, leaf, or butter lettuce)
- **Tomato:** 1, sliced
- **Red Onion:** 1/4, thinly sliced (optional)
- **Mayonnaise:** 2 tbsp
- **Mustard:** 1 tbsp (optional)
- **Salt and Pepper:** To taste
- **Olive Oil:** 1 tbsp (optional, for toasting the bread)

Instructions:

1. **Prepare the Ingredients:**
   - Slice the avocado, tomato, and red onion (if using). Season the avocado slices with a little salt and pepper if desired.
2. **Toast the Bread (Optional):**
   - For a crispy sandwich, you can toast the bread slices. Heat olive oil in a skillet over medium heat. Toast each slice of bread until golden brown and crispy.
3. **Prepare the Spreads:**
   - Spread mayonnaise on one side of each slice of bread. If you like, spread mustard on one side of each slice as well.
4. **Assemble the Sandwich:**
   - On one slice of bread, layer the sliced turkey breast.
   - Add slices of avocado on top of the turkey.
   - Follow with lettuce leaves and tomato slices. Add red onion if using.
   - Season with a little salt and pepper to taste.
   - Top with the second slice of bread, mayonnaise side down.
5. **Serve:**
   - Cut the sandwich in half if desired and serve immediately.

Enjoy your fresh and satisfying Turkey and Avocado Sandwich!

Meatball Sub

Ingredients:

For the Meatballs:

- **Ground Beef:** 1 lb
- **Breadcrumbs:** 1/2 cup
- **Parmesan Cheese:** 1/4 cup, grated
- **Egg:** 1
- **Garlic:** 2 cloves, minced
- **Parsley:** 2 tbsp, chopped (fresh or 1 tbsp dried)
- **Salt:** 1 tsp
- **Black Pepper:** 1/2 tsp
- **Italian Seasoning:** 1/2 tsp

For the Sauce:

- **Olive Oil:** 1 tbsp
- **Garlic:** 2 cloves, minced
- **Canned Tomato Sauce:** 2 cups
- **Canned Diced Tomatoes:** 1 cup
- **Sugar:** 1 tsp (optional, to balance acidity)
- **Basil:** 1 tsp, dried (or 2 tsp fresh, chopped)
- **Oregano:** 1/2 tsp
- **Salt and Pepper:** To taste

For Assembling:

- **Sub Rolls:** 4
- **Mozzarella Cheese:** 1 cup, shredded
- **Parmesan Cheese:** 1/4 cup, grated
- **Fresh Basil or Parsley:** For garnish (optional)

Instructions:

1. **Prepare the Meatballs:**
   - Preheat your oven to 375°F (190°C).
   - In a large bowl, combine ground beef, breadcrumbs, Parmesan cheese, egg, minced garlic, parsley, salt, pepper, and Italian seasoning. Mix until well combined but do not overmix.
   - Shape the mixture into 1 to 1.5-inch meatballs and place them on a baking sheet lined with parchment paper.
2. **Bake the Meatballs:**

- Bake in the preheated oven for 15-20 minutes, or until cooked through (internal temperature should reach 160°F or 71°C). Remove from the oven and set aside.

3. **Prepare the Sauce:**
    - While the meatballs are baking, heat olive oil in a large skillet over medium heat.
    - Add minced garlic and cook for about 1 minute, or until fragrant.
    - Stir in the tomato sauce and diced tomatoes. Add sugar, basil, oregano, salt, and pepper. Simmer for 10-15 minutes to let the flavors meld together.

4. **Combine Meatballs and Sauce:**
    - Add the baked meatballs to the sauce and gently simmer for an additional 5-10 minutes, allowing the meatballs to absorb some of the sauce flavor.

5. **Assemble the Subs:**
    - Preheat your oven's broiler.
    - Slice the sub rolls lengthwise, but not all the way through, to create a pocket.
    - Spoon a few meatballs and sauce into each roll.
    - Top with shredded mozzarella cheese and a sprinkle of grated Parmesan cheese.

6. **Broil the Subs:**
    - Place the filled subs under the broiler for 2-4 minutes, or until the cheese is melted and bubbly. Watch closely to avoid burning.

7. **Serve:**
    - Remove from the oven and garnish with fresh basil or parsley if desired.
    - Serve immediately and enjoy your hearty and flavorful Meatball Subs!

BLT Sandwich

Ingredients:

- **Bread:** 4 slices (white, whole wheat, or sourdough), toasted
- **Bacon:** 8 slices
- **Lettuce:** 4 leaves (romaine, iceberg, or butter lettuce)
- **Tomato:** 1 large, sliced
- **Mayonnaise:** 2 tbsp
- **Salt and Pepper:** To taste

Instructions:

1. **Cook the Bacon:**
   - Heat a skillet over medium heat. Add the bacon slices and cook until crispy, about 4-6 minutes per side.
   - Remove the bacon from the skillet and drain on paper towels to remove excess grease.
2. **Prepare the Bread:**
   - While the bacon is cooking, toast the bread slices until golden brown.
3. **Assemble the Sandwich:**
   - Spread mayonnaise on one side of each slice of toasted bread.
   - On the mayo side of two slices, layer the lettuce leaves, followed by the tomato slices. Season the tomato with a little salt and pepper.
   - Place the crispy bacon on top of the tomatoes.
   - Top with the remaining slices of toasted bread, mayo side down.
4. **Serve:**
   - Cut the sandwiches in half diagonally if desired.
   - Serve immediately with your favorite side, such as chips, pickles, or a small salad.

Enjoy your classic BLT Sandwich, simple yet full of flavor!

Chicken Caesar Wrap

Ingredients:

- **Chicken Breasts:** 2 boneless, skinless
- **Olive Oil:** 2 tbsp
- **Salt and Pepper:** To taste
- **Romaine Lettuce:** 2 cups, chopped
- **Parmesan Cheese:** 1/4 cup, grated
- **Croutons:** 1/2 cup, crushed (optional)
- **Caesar Dressing:** 1/2 cup (store-bought or homemade)
- **Large Flour Tortillas:** 4

For Homemade Caesar Dressing (optional):

- **Mayonnaise:** 1/2 cup
- **Parmesan Cheese:** 1/4 cup, grated
- **Garlic:** 1 clove, minced
- **Lemon Juice:** 1 tbsp
- **Anchovy Paste:** 1 tsp (optional)
- **Dijon Mustard:** 1 tsp
- **Worcestershire Sauce:** 1 tsp
- **Salt and Pepper:** To taste

Instructions:

1. **Prepare the Chicken:**
    - Preheat your grill or skillet over medium-high heat.
    - Brush the chicken breasts with olive oil and season with salt and pepper.
    - Grill or cook the chicken for 6-8 minutes per side, or until the internal temperature reaches 165°F (74°C) and the juices run clear. Let the chicken rest for a few minutes before slicing or chopping into bite-sized pieces.
2. **Make the Caesar Dressing (if homemade):**
    - In a bowl, whisk together mayonnaise, Parmesan cheese, minced garlic, lemon juice, anchovy paste (if using), Dijon mustard, Worcestershire sauce, salt, and pepper until smooth.
3. **Prepare the Wrap Ingredients:**
    - In a large bowl, combine the chopped romaine lettuce, Parmesan cheese, and crushed croutons (if using).
    - Add the Caesar dressing to the lettuce mixture and toss until well coated.
4. **Assemble the Wraps:**
    - Warm the flour tortillas in a skillet or microwave until pliable.
    - Spread some Caesar dressing on each tortilla if you like extra flavor.

- Evenly distribute the dressed lettuce mixture among the tortillas.
- Add the sliced or chopped grilled chicken on top of the lettuce mixture.
5. **Wrap It Up:**
    - Fold in the sides of each tortilla, then roll it up tightly from the bottom to enclose the filling.
6. **Serve:**
    - Slice the wraps in half if desired. Serve immediately or wrap tightly in foil for a convenient on-the-go lunch.

Enjoy your delicious Chicken Caesar Wrap, packed with flavor and perfect for a quick meal!

Sloppy Joes

Ingredients:

- **Ground Beef:** 1 lb
- **Onion:** 1 medium, finely chopped
- **Green Bell Pepper:** 1, finely chopped
- **Garlic:** 2 cloves, minced
- **Tomato Sauce:** 1 cup
- **Ketchup:** 1/2 cup
- **Yellow Mustard:** 1 tbsp
- **Worcestershire Sauce:** 1 tbsp
- **Brown Sugar:** 1 tbsp
- **Paprika:** 1 tsp
- **Chili Powder:** 1 tsp
- **Salt:** 1/2 tsp
- **Black Pepper:** 1/4 tsp
- **Red Pepper Flakes:** 1/4 tsp (optional, for heat)
- **Hamburger Buns:** 4, toasted

Instructions:

1. **Cook the Meat:**
   - In a large skillet over medium heat, cook the ground beef until browned, breaking it apart with a spoon as it cooks. Drain any excess fat.
2. **Add Vegetables:**
   - Add the chopped onion, green bell pepper, and minced garlic to the skillet with the beef. Cook until the vegetables are softened, about 5 minutes.
3. **Prepare the Sauce:**
   - Stir in the tomato sauce, ketchup, mustard, Worcestershire sauce, and brown sugar. Mix well.
   - Add paprika, chili powder, salt, pepper, and red pepper flakes (if using). Stir to combine.
4. **Simmer:**
   - Reduce the heat to low and let the mixture simmer for 10-15 minutes, stirring occasionally. The sauce should thicken and the flavors should meld together.
5. **Toast the Buns:**
   - While the meat mixture is simmering, toast the hamburger buns in a skillet or oven until golden brown.
6. **Assemble the Sloppy Joes:**
   - Spoon the hot beef mixture onto the bottom half of each toasted bun. Top with the other half of the bun.
7. **Serve:**

    - Serve immediately with your favorite side dishes, such as pickles, coleslaw, or potato chips.

Enjoy your hearty and flavorful Sloppy Joes!

BBQ Chicken Pizza

Ingredients:

For the Pizza:

- **Pizza Dough:** 1 lb (store-bought or homemade)
- **Cooked Chicken:** 1 cup, shredded or chopped (grilled or rotisserie chicken works well)
- **BBQ Sauce:** 1/2 cup (your favorite brand or homemade)
- **Red Onion:** 1/2, thinly sliced
- **Mozzarella Cheese:** 1 cup, shredded
- **Cheddar Cheese:** 1/2 cup, shredded
- **Cilantro:** 1/4 cup, chopped (optional, for garnish)

For Homemade BBQ Sauce (optional):

- **Ketchup:** 1/2 cup
- **Brown Sugar:** 1/4 cup
- **Apple Cider Vinegar:** 2 tbsp
- **Worcestershire Sauce:** 1 tbsp
- **Paprika:** 1 tsp
- **Garlic Powder:** 1/2 tsp
- **Onion Powder:** 1/2 tsp
- **Salt and Pepper:** To taste

Instructions:

1. **Preheat the Oven:**
   - Preheat your oven to 475°F (245°C). If using a pizza stone, place it in the oven to preheat as well.
2. **Prepare the Pizza Dough:**
   - Roll out the pizza dough on a floured surface to your desired thickness. Transfer to a pizza peel or a baking sheet lined with parchment paper if not using a pizza stone.
3. **Prepare the BBQ Sauce (if homemade):**
   - In a small saucepan, combine ketchup, brown sugar, apple cider vinegar, Worcestershire sauce, paprika, garlic powder, onion powder, salt, and pepper.
   - Simmer over medium heat for 5-10 minutes, stirring occasionally, until the sauce thickens. Allow it to cool slightly.
4. **Assemble the Pizza:**
   - Spread a thin layer of BBQ sauce over the pizza dough, leaving a small border around the edges.
   - Scatter the shredded or chopped chicken evenly over the sauce.
   - Top with thin slices of red onion.

- Sprinkle mozzarella cheese and cheddar cheese over the top.
5. **Bake the Pizza:**
    - Bake in the preheated oven for 12-15 minutes, or until the crust is golden and the cheese is bubbly and melted.
6. **Garnish and Serve:**
    - Remove the pizza from the oven and let it cool slightly.
    - Garnish with chopped cilantro if desired.
    - Slice and serve hot.

Enjoy your flavorful BBQ Chicken Pizza!

Spinach and Artichoke Dip with Chips

Ingredients:

- **Frozen Spinach:** 10 oz, thawed and drained
- **Canned Artichoke Hearts:** 14 oz, drained and chopped
- **Cream Cheese:** 8 oz, softened
- **Sour Cream:** 1/2 cup
- **Mayonnaise:** 1/2 cup
- **Parmesan Cheese:** 1/2 cup, grated
- **Mozzarella Cheese:** 1/2 cup, shredded
- **Garlic:** 2 cloves, minced
- **Salt:** 1/2 tsp
- **Black Pepper:** 1/4 tsp
- **Red Pepper Flakes:** 1/4 tsp (optional, for a bit of heat)
- **Olive Oil:** 1 tbsp (for greasing the baking dish)

For Serving:

- **Chips:** Tortilla chips, pita chips, or your favorite dipping chips

Instructions:

1. **Preheat the Oven:**
   - Preheat your oven to 375°F (190°C).
2. **Prepare the Dip:**
   - In a large bowl, combine the softened cream cheese, sour cream, and mayonnaise until smooth.
   - Stir in the grated Parmesan cheese, shredded mozzarella cheese, and minced garlic.
   - Add the chopped spinach and artichoke hearts to the mixture. Mix well until all ingredients are evenly combined.
   - Season with salt, black pepper, and red pepper flakes (if using).
3. **Bake the Dip:**
   - Lightly grease a baking dish with olive oil (an 8x8 inch dish or similar size works well).
   - Spread the spinach and artichoke mixture evenly in the prepared dish.
   - Bake in the preheated oven for 25-30 minutes, or until the dip is bubbly and the top is golden brown.
4. **Serve:**
   - Remove the dip from the oven and let it cool slightly before serving.
   - Serve warm with tortilla chips, pita chips, or your favorite dipping chips.

Enjoy your creamy and flavorful Spinach and Artichoke Dip with crispy chips!

Chicken Quesadilla

Ingredients:

- **Chicken Breasts:** 2 boneless, skinless, cooked and shredded
- **Flour Tortillas:** 4 large
- **Shredded Cheese:** 1 cup (cheddar, Monterey Jack, or a blend)
- **Olive Oil or Butter:** 2 tbsp (for cooking)
- **Bell Peppers:** 1, thinly sliced (optional)
- **Onion:** 1/2, thinly sliced (optional)
- **Garlic Powder:** 1/2 tsp
- **Cumin:** 1/2 tsp
- **Paprika:** 1/2 tsp
- **Salt and Pepper:** To taste
- **Sour Cream:** For serving
- **Salsa:** For serving
- **Chopped Cilantro:** For garnish (optional)

Instructions:

1. **Prepare the Chicken:**
   - If not already cooked, cook the chicken breasts in a skillet over medium heat until fully cooked (about 6-8 minutes per side). Let cool slightly, then shred with two forks.
2. **Season the Chicken:**
   - In a bowl, combine the shredded chicken with garlic powder, cumin, paprika, salt, and pepper. Mix well.
3. **Prepare the Vegetables (Optional):**
   - If using bell peppers and onion, heat a skillet over medium heat with a little olive oil. Add the sliced vegetables and cook until softened, about 5 minutes. Set aside.
4. **Assemble the Quesadillas:**
   - Heat a large skillet over medium heat and add 1 tablespoon of olive oil or butter.
   - Place one tortilla in the skillet. Sprinkle half of the shredded cheese evenly over the tortilla.
   - Spread half of the seasoned chicken (and vegetables, if using) over the cheese.
   - Top with another tortilla. Cook for about 2-3 minutes, or until the bottom tortilla is golden brown and the cheese is starting to melt.
   - Carefully flip the quesadilla and cook for another 2-3 minutes on the other side until golden brown and the cheese is fully melted.
5. **Repeat:**
   - Repeat the process with the remaining tortillas, cheese, chicken, and optional vegetables.

6. **Serve:**
    - Remove the quesadillas from the skillet and let them cool for a minute before slicing into wedges.
    - Serve with sour cream, salsa, and chopped cilantro if desired.

Enjoy your tasty and cheesy Chicken Quesadillas!

Buffalo Chicken Salad

Ingredients:

For the Chicken:

- **Chicken Breasts:** 2 boneless, skinless
- **Buffalo Sauce:** 1/2 cup (your favorite brand or homemade)
- **Olive Oil:** 1 tbsp (for cooking)

For the Salad:

- **Romaine Lettuce:** 4 cups, chopped
- **Cherry Tomatoes:** 1 cup, halved
- **Cucumber:** 1, sliced
- **Red Onion:** 1/4, thinly sliced
- **Celery:** 2 stalks, sliced
- **Carrots:** 1 cup, shredded
- **Blue Cheese Crumbles:** 1/4 cup (optional)
- **Ranch or Blue Cheese Dressing:** For serving

Instructions:

1. **Cook the Chicken:**
   - Heat olive oil in a skillet over medium heat.
   - Season the chicken breasts with salt and pepper.
   - Cook the chicken for 6-8 minutes per side, or until fully cooked and the internal temperature reaches 165°F (74°C).
   - Let the chicken rest for a few minutes, then slice or shred it.
2. **Prepare the Buffalo Sauce:**
   - Toss the cooked chicken in buffalo sauce until well coated. You can adjust the amount of sauce to your taste.
3. **Prepare the Salad:**
   - In a large bowl, combine the chopped romaine lettuce, cherry tomatoes, cucumber, red onion, celery, and shredded carrots.
4. **Assemble the Salad:**
   - Top the salad with the buffalo chicken.
   - Sprinkle with blue cheese crumbles if desired.
5. **Serve:**
   - Serve the salad with ranch or blue cheese dressing on the side, or drizzle it over the top.

Enjoy your spicy and refreshing Buffalo Chicken Salad!

Grilled Portobello Mushroom Burger

Ingredients:

- **Portobello Mushrooms:** 4 large caps, stems removed
- **Olive Oil:** 2 tbsp
- **Balsamic Vinegar:** 2 tbsp
- **Garlic:** 2 cloves, minced
- **Salt:** 1/2 tsp
- **Black Pepper:** 1/4 tsp
- **Dried Oregano:** 1/2 tsp
- **Burger Buns:** 4, toasted
- **Lettuce:** 4 leaves (romaine, butter, or your choice)
- **Tomato:** 1 large, sliced
- **Red Onion:** 1 small, sliced
- **Cheese:** 4 slices (optional, such as Swiss, cheddar, or provolone)
- **Mayonnaise:** 2 tbsp (optional, for spreading on buns)
- **Mustard or Ketchup:** Optional, for serving

Instructions:

1. **Prepare the Marinade:**
    - In a small bowl, whisk together olive oil, balsamic vinegar, minced garlic, salt, black pepper, and dried oregano.
2. **Marinate the Mushrooms:**
    - Place the portobello mushroom caps in a shallow dish or a large resealable bag.
    - Pour the marinade over the mushrooms and let them marinate for at least 15-30 minutes.
3. **Preheat the Grill:**
    - Preheat your grill to medium-high heat.
4. **Grill the Mushrooms:**
    - Remove the mushrooms from the marinade and place them on the grill.
    - Grill the mushrooms for about 4-5 minutes per side, or until tender and well-marked by grill lines. If using cheese, add a slice on top of each mushroom during the last minute of grilling and close the grill lid to melt the cheese.
5. **Prepare the Buns:**
    - While the mushrooms are grilling, toast the burger buns on the grill or in a toaster until golden brown.
6. **Assemble the Burgers:**
    - Spread mayonnaise on the bottom half of each toasted bun if desired.
    - Place a grilled portobello mushroom cap on each bun.
    - Top with lettuce, tomato slices, and red onion.
    - Add mustard or ketchup if desired.

- Place the top half of the bun on the burger.
7. **Serve:**
    - Serve the Grilled Portobello Mushroom Burgers immediately, with your favorite side dishes like sweet potato fries, chips, or a simple salad.

Enjoy your hearty and satisfying Grilled Portobello Mushroom Burger!

Lobster Roll

Ingredients:

For the Lobster Salad:

- **Lobster Meat:** 1 lb, cooked and chopped (from about 2 medium lobsters, or pre-cooked lobster meat)
- **Mayonnaise:** 1/4 cup
- **Lemon Juice:** 1 tbsp
- **Celery:** 1 stalk, finely diced
- **Chives or Green Onions:** 2 tbsp, finely chopped
- **Salt:** 1/4 tsp
- **Black Pepper:** 1/4 tsp
- **Paprika:** 1/4 tsp (optional)

For the Rolls:

- **New England-style Hot Dog Buns:** 4
- **Butter:** 2 tbsp, softened (for toasting the buns)
- **Lettuce:** 4 leaves (optional, for lining the buns)

Instructions:

1. **Prepare the Lobster Salad:**
   - In a bowl, combine the chopped lobster meat, mayonnaise, lemon juice, diced celery, and chopped chives or green onions.
   - Season with salt, black pepper, and paprika (if using). Mix until well combined.
   - Chill in the refrigerator while you prepare the buns.
2. **Toast the Buns:**
   - Heat a skillet or griddle over medium heat.
   - Spread softened butter on the outside of each hot dog bun.
   - Toast the buns in the skillet until golden brown and crisp, about 2-3 minutes per side.
3. **Assemble the Lobster Rolls:**
   - If using, line each toasted bun with a leaf of lettuce to help catch the lobster salad and add some freshness.
   - Spoon the chilled lobster salad into each toasted bun, filling generously.
4. **Serve:**
   - Serve the Lobster Rolls immediately, with lemon wedges on the side if desired.

Enjoy your classic and luxurious Lobster Rolls!

Black Bean Burger

Ingredients:

- **Canned Black Beans:** 1 can (15 oz), drained and rinsed
- **Breadcrumbs:** 1/2 cup (use gluten-free if needed)
- **Egg:** 1 large (or a flax egg for a vegan option)
- **Onion:** 1 small, finely chopped
- **Garlic:** 2 cloves, minced
- **Red Bell Pepper:** 1/2, finely chopped
- **Cilantro:** 1/4 cup, chopped (optional)
- **Cumin:** 1/2 tsp
- **Paprika:** 1/2 tsp
- **Chili Powder:** 1/2 tsp
- **Salt:** 1/2 tsp
- **Black Pepper:** 1/4 tsp
- **Olive Oil:** 2 tbsp (for cooking)

For Serving:

- **Burger Buns:** 4, toasted
- **Lettuce:** 4 leaves
- **Tomato:** 1, sliced
- **Avocado:** 1, sliced
- **Red Onion:** 1/2, sliced
- **Ketchup, Mustard, or Your Favorite Sauce:** For topping

Instructions:

1. **Prepare the Bean Mixture:**
    - In a large bowl, mash the black beans with a fork or potato masher, leaving some chunks for texture.
    - Add the breadcrumbs, egg, chopped onion, minced garlic, chopped red bell pepper, cilantro (if using), cumin, paprika, chili powder, salt, and black pepper. Mix well until everything is combined.
2. **Form the Patties:**
    - Divide the mixture into 4 equal portions and shape each portion into a patty about 1/2 inch thick.
3. **Cook the Patties:**
    - Heat olive oil in a skillet over medium heat.
    - Cook the patties for about 5-6 minutes on each side, or until they are golden brown and crispy on the outside. Be careful when flipping as the patties can be delicate.

4. **Prepare the Buns:**
   - While the patties are cooking, toast the burger buns in a toaster or on a skillet until golden brown.
5. **Assemble the Burgers:**
   - Place each cooked black bean patty on the bottom half of a toasted bun.
   - Top with lettuce, tomato slices, avocado slices, and red onion.
   - Add ketchup, mustard, or your favorite sauce as desired.
   - Cover with the top half of the bun.
6. **Serve:**
   - Serve the Black Bean Burgers immediately, with your favorite side dishes like sweet potato fries or a simple salad.

Enjoy your tasty and satisfying Black Bean Burgers!

Chicken Fried Rice

Ingredients:

- **Chicken Breasts:** 2 boneless, skinless, diced
- **Olive Oil or Vegetable Oil:** 2 tbsp
- **Garlic:** 2 cloves, minced
- **Ginger:** 1 tbsp, minced (optional)
- **Carrots:** 1 cup, diced
- **Frozen Peas:** 1/2 cup
- **Green Onions:** 3, sliced
- **Cooked Rice:** 3 cups (preferably cold or day-old)
- **Soy Sauce:** 3 tbsp (or to taste)
- **Sesame Oil:** 1 tbsp (optional, for flavor)
- **Eggs:** 2, lightly beaten
- **Salt and Pepper:** To taste

Instructions:

1. **Cook the Chicken:**
    - Heat 1 tablespoon of oil in a large skillet or wok over medium-high heat.
    - Add the diced chicken and cook until fully cooked and no longer pink in the center, about 5-7 minutes. Remove from the skillet and set aside.
2. **Prepare the Vegetables:**
    - In the same skillet, add the remaining 1 tablespoon of oil.
    - Add the minced garlic and ginger (if using) and sauté for about 30 seconds until fragrant.
    - Add the diced carrots and cook for 3-4 minutes until they start to soften.
    - Stir in the frozen peas and cook for an additional 2 minutes.
3. **Add the Rice:**
    - Push the vegetables to one side of the skillet. Add the cold or day-old rice to the empty side of the skillet. Use a spatula to break up any clumps and cook for a few minutes until the rice is heated through.
4. **Add the Chicken:**
    - Add the cooked chicken back to the skillet. Mix well with the rice and vegetables.
5. **Season and Scramble the Eggs:**
    - Push the rice mixture to one side of the skillet again. Pour the beaten eggs into the empty side and scramble until fully cooked, then mix into the rice.
    - Add soy sauce, sesame oil (if using), and season with salt and pepper to taste. Mix well to combine everything evenly.
6. **Finish and Serve:**
    - Stir in the sliced green onions and cook for an additional minute.
    - Serve hot, straight from the skillet.

Enjoy your homemade Chicken Fried Rice!

Macaroni and Cheese

Ingredients:

- **Elbow Macaroni:** 2 cups (dry)
- **Butter:** 4 tbsp
- **All-Purpose Flour:** 1/4 cup
- **Milk:** 2 cups (whole milk preferred)
- **Cheddar Cheese:** 2 cups, shredded (sharp or mild, depending on preference)
- **Monterey Jack Cheese:** 1 cup, shredded (optional, for extra creaminess)
- **Salt:** 1/2 tsp
- **Black Pepper:** 1/4 tsp
- **Paprika:** 1/4 tsp
- **Mustard Powder:** 1/4 tsp (optional, for added depth)
- **Breadcrumbs:** 1/2 cup (for topping, optional)
- **Parmesan Cheese:** 1/4 cup, grated (for topping, optional)

Instructions:

1. **Cook the Macaroni:**
   - Cook the elbow macaroni according to package instructions until al dente. Drain and set aside.
2. **Prepare the Cheese Sauce:**
   - In a large saucepan, melt the butter over medium heat.
   - Add the flour and whisk continuously for about 1-2 minutes to create a roux. This helps thicken the sauce.
   - Gradually add the milk, whisking constantly to avoid lumps. Continue to cook and whisk until the sauce thickens and starts to bubble, about 5 minutes.
3. **Add the Cheese:**
   - Reduce the heat to low and stir in the shredded cheddar cheese and Monterey Jack cheese (if using). Continue to stir until the cheese is completely melted and the sauce is smooth.
   - Season with salt, black pepper, paprika, and mustard powder (if using). Adjust seasoning to taste.
4. **Combine Pasta and Sauce:**
   - Add the cooked macaroni to the cheese sauce, stirring to coat the pasta evenly.
5. **Optional: Bake for a Crispy Topping:**
   - Preheat your oven to 350°F (175°C).
   - Transfer the macaroni and cheese to a greased baking dish.
   - In a small bowl, mix the breadcrumbs with the grated Parmesan cheese. Sprinkle this mixture evenly over the top of the macaroni and cheese.
   - Bake in the preheated oven for 20-25 minutes, or until the top is golden brown and crispy.

6. **Serve:**
    - Allow the macaroni and cheese to cool for a few minutes before serving.

Enjoy your creamy, cheesy, and comforting Macaroni and Cheese!

Beef Chili

Ingredients:

- **Ground Beef:** 1 lb
- **Olive Oil:** 1 tbsp
- **Onion:** 1 large, chopped
- **Garlic:** 3 cloves, minced
- **Green Bell Pepper:** 1, chopped
- **Red Bell Pepper:** 1, chopped
- **Carrots:** 2, peeled and diced
- **Celery:** 2 stalks, diced
- **Tomato Paste:** 2 tbsp
- **Diced Tomatoes:** 1 can (14.5 oz)
- **Kidney Beans:** 1 can (15 oz), drained and rinsed
- **Black Beans:** 1 can (15 oz), drained and rinsed
- **Beef Broth:** 2 cups
- **Chili Powder:** 2 tbsp
- **Cumin:** 1 tsp
- **Paprika:** 1 tsp
- **Oregano:** 1 tsp
- **Salt:** 1 tsp (or to taste)
- **Black Pepper:** 1/2 tsp
- **Red Pepper Flakes:** 1/4 tsp (optional, for heat)
- **Bay Leaf:** 1 (optional)

For Serving:

- **Shredded Cheese:** For topping (optional)
- **Sour Cream:** For topping (optional)
- **Chopped Green Onions:** For garnish (optional)
- **Crushed Tortilla Chips or Cornbread:** For serving

Instructions:

1. **Cook the Beef:**
   - In a large pot or Dutch oven, heat the olive oil over medium heat.
   - Add the ground beef and cook until browned, breaking it apart with a spoon. Drain excess fat if needed.
2. **Sauté Vegetables:**
   - Add the chopped onion, minced garlic, green bell pepper, red bell pepper, carrots, and celery to the pot.
   - Cook until the vegetables are softened, about 5-7 minutes.

3. **Add Tomato Paste and Spices:**
    - Stir in the tomato paste and cook for 2 minutes.
    - Add the chili powder, cumin, paprika, oregano, salt, black pepper, and red pepper flakes (if using). Mix well.
4. **Add Tomatoes and Beans:**
    - Add the diced tomatoes, kidney beans, black beans, and beef broth.
    - Stir to combine and bring to a simmer.
5. **Simmer the Chili:**
    - Add the bay leaf (if using).
    - Reduce the heat to low and let the chili simmer uncovered for 30-40 minutes, stirring occasionally. This allows the flavors to meld together and the chili to thicken.
6. **Adjust Seasoning:**
    - Taste and adjust seasoning as needed. Remove the bay leaf before serving.
7. **Serve:**
    - Ladle the chili into bowls and top with shredded cheese, sour cream, and chopped green onions if desired.
    - Serve with crushed tortilla chips or cornbread on the side.

Enjoy your hearty and satisfying Beef Chili!

Nachos

Ingredients:

- **Tortilla Chips:** 10-12 cups (store-bought or homemade)
- **Ground Beef:** 1 lb (or use shredded chicken or pork)
- **Taco Seasoning:** 1 packet (or homemade seasoning blend)
- **Cheddar Cheese:** 2 cups, shredded
- **Monterey Jack Cheese:** 1 cup, shredded (optional, for extra creaminess)
- **Black Beans:** 1 can (15 oz), drained and rinsed
- **Corn Kernels:** 1 cup (fresh, frozen, or canned)
- **Green Onions:** 2-3, sliced
- **Tomato:** 1-2, diced
- **Jalapeños:** 1-2, sliced (optional, for heat)
- **Sour Cream:** For serving
- **Salsa:** For serving
- **Guacamole:** For serving
- **Chopped Cilantro:** For garnish (optional)
- **Lime Wedges:** For serving (optional)

Instructions:

1. **Prepare the Meat:**
    - In a skillet over medium heat, cook the ground beef until browned, breaking it apart with a spoon.
    - Drain excess fat if needed.
    - Add the taco seasoning and a splash of water (about 1/4 cup). Stir and cook for an additional 2-3 minutes until the seasoning is well incorporated and the meat is evenly coated. Set aside.
2. **Preheat the Oven:**
    - Preheat your oven to 375°F (190°C).
3. **Assemble the Nachos:**
    - On a large baking sheet or oven-safe platter, spread out a layer of tortilla chips.
    - Evenly distribute the seasoned ground beef over the chips.
    - Sprinkle black beans, corn kernels, and a mix of cheddar and Monterey Jack cheese over the top.
    - Add a few jalapeño slices if you like it spicy.
4. **Bake the Nachos:**
    - Bake in the preheated oven for 10-12 minutes, or until the cheese is melted and bubbly. Keep an eye on them to avoid burning.
5. **Add Fresh Toppings:**
    - Remove from the oven and immediately top with diced tomatoes, sliced green onions, and any additional fresh toppings you like.

6. **Serve:**
    - Serve the nachos with side dishes like sour cream, salsa, guacamole, and lime wedges.
    - Garnish with chopped cilantro if desired.

Enjoy your cheesy, crunchy, and delicious Nachos!

Cornbread and Chili

Ingredients:

- **Ground Beef:** 1 lb
- **Olive Oil:** 1 tbsp
- **Onion:** 1 large, chopped
- **Garlic:** 3 cloves, minced
- **Green Bell Pepper:** 1, chopped
- **Red Bell Pepper:** 1, chopped
- **Carrots:** 2, peeled and diced
- **Celery:** 2 stalks, diced
- **Tomato Paste:** 2 tbsp
- **Diced Tomatoes:** 1 can (14.5 oz)
- **Kidney Beans:** 1 can (15 oz), drained and rinsed
- **Black Beans:** 1 can (15 oz), drained and rinsed
- **Beef Broth:** 2 cups
- **Chili Powder:** 2 tbsp
- **Cumin:** 1 tsp
- **Paprika:** 1 tsp
- **Oregano:** 1 tsp
- **Salt:** 1 tsp (or to taste)
- **Black Pepper:** 1/2 tsp
- **Red Pepper Flakes:** 1/4 tsp (optional, for heat)
- **Bay Leaf:** 1 (optional)

For Serving:

- **Shredded Cheese:** For topping (optional)
- **Sour Cream:** For topping (optional)
- **Chopped Green Onions:** For garnish (optional)
- **Cornbread:** Recipe follows

Instructions:

1. **Cook the Beef:**
    - Heat olive oil in a large pot or Dutch oven over medium heat.
    - Add the ground beef and cook until browned, breaking it apart with a spoon. Drain excess fat if needed.
2. **Sauté Vegetables:**
    - Add chopped onion, minced garlic, green bell pepper, red bell pepper, carrots, and celery.
    - Cook until vegetables are softened, about 5-7 minutes.

3. **Add Tomato Paste and Spices:**
   - Stir in the tomato paste and cook for 2 minutes.
   - Add chili powder, cumin, paprika, oregano, salt, black pepper, and red pepper flakes (if using). Mix well.
4. **Add Tomatoes and Beans:**
   - Stir in diced tomatoes, kidney beans, black beans, and beef broth.
   - Bring to a boil, then reduce heat and let simmer for 30-40 minutes, stirring occasionally. Add bay leaf if using.
5. **Adjust Seasoning:**
   - Taste and adjust seasoning as needed. Remove bay leaf before serving.
6. **Serve:**
   - Ladle chili into bowls and top with shredded cheese, sour cream, and chopped green onions if desired.

Cornbread Recipe

Ingredients:

- **Cornmeal:** 1 cup
- **All-Purpose Flour:** 1 cup
- **Sugar:** 1/4 cup
- **Baking Powder:** 1 tbsp
- **Salt:** 1/2 tsp
- **Egg:** 1 large
- **Milk:** 1 cup
- **Butter:** 1/4 cup, melted

Instructions:

1. **Preheat Oven:**
   - Preheat your oven to 400°F (200°C). Grease an 8-inch square baking dish or a cast-iron skillet.
2. **Mix Dry Ingredients:**
   - In a large bowl, whisk together cornmeal, flour, sugar, baking powder, and salt.
3. **Mix Wet Ingredients:**
   - In another bowl, whisk together the egg, milk, and melted butter.
4. **Combine:**
   - Pour the wet ingredients into the dry ingredients and stir until just combined. Do not overmix.
5. **Bake:**
   - Pour the batter into the prepared baking dish or skillet. Bake in the preheated oven for 20-25 minutes, or until the top is golden brown and a toothpick inserted into the center comes out clean.
6. **Serve:**

    - Allow the cornbread to cool slightly before cutting into squares. Serve warm with your chili.

Enjoy your comforting meal of Beef Chili and Cornbread!

Sweet and Sour Chicken

Ingredients:

- **Cornmeal:** 1 cup
- **All-Purpose Flour:** 1 cup
- **Sugar:** 1/4 cup
- **Baking Powder:** 1 tbsp
- **Salt:** 1/2 tsp
- **Egg:** 1 large
- **Milk:** 1 cup
- **Butter:** 1/4 cup, melted

Instructions:

1. **Preheat Oven:**
   - Preheat your oven to 400°F (200°C). Grease an 8-inch square baking dish or a cast-iron skillet.
2. **Mix Dry Ingredients:**
   - In a large bowl, whisk together cornmeal, flour, sugar, baking powder, and salt.
3. **Mix Wet Ingredients:**
   - In another bowl, whisk together the egg, milk, and melted butter.
4. **Combine:**
   - Pour the wet ingredients into the dry ingredients and stir until just combined. Do not overmix.
5. **Bake:**
   - Pour the batter into the prepared baking dish or skillet. Bake in the preheated oven for 20-25 minutes, or until the top is golden brown and a toothpick inserted into the center comes out clean.
6. **Serve:**
   - Allow the cornbread to cool slightly before cutting into squares. Serve warm with your chili.

Enjoy your comforting meal of Beef Chili and Cornbread!

Philly Cheesesteak Pizza

Ingredients:

For the Pizza Dough:

- **Pizza Dough:** 1 lb (store-bought or homemade)
    - If making homemade, you'll need 2 1/4 tsp active dry yeast, 1 1/2 cups warm water, 3 1/2 cups all-purpose flour, 2 tbsp olive oil, 1 tsp sugar, and 1 tsp salt.

For the Topping:

- **Beef Sirloin or Ribeye:** 1/2 lb, thinly sliced
- **Olive Oil:** 1 tbsp (for cooking the beef)
- **Onion:** 1 medium, thinly sliced
- **Bell Peppers:** 1 green and 1 red, thinly sliced
- **Mushrooms:** 1 cup, sliced (optional)
- **Garlic:** 2 cloves, minced
- **Provolone Cheese:** 1 cup, shredded
- **Mozzarella Cheese:** 1 cup, shredded
- **Salt:** 1/2 tsp
- **Black Pepper:** 1/4 tsp
- **Oregano:** 1/2 tsp
- **Red Pepper Flakes:** 1/4 tsp (optional, for heat)

For the Pizza Sauce (optional):

- **Olive Oil:** 1 tbsp
- **Garlic:** 1 clove, minced
- **Tomato Sauce:** 1/2 cup
- **Dried Oregano:** 1/2 tsp
- **Salt:** 1/4 tsp
- **Black Pepper:** 1/4 tsp

Instructions:

1. **Prepare the Pizza Dough:**
    - If using store-bought dough, follow the instructions on the package for preheating the oven and preparing the dough.
    - For homemade dough, mix yeast and sugar with warm water, let it sit for 5 minutes. Combine flour and salt in a bowl, add yeast mixture and olive oil, and knead until smooth. Let rise for about 1-2 hours or until doubled in size.
2. **Cook the Beef:**
    - Heat olive oil in a skillet over medium-high heat.

- Add the thinly sliced beef and cook until browned, about 3-4 minutes.
- Add minced garlic, and sliced onion, bell peppers, and mushrooms (if using). Cook until vegetables are tender and beef is cooked through. Season with salt, black pepper, and oregano. Set aside.

3. **Prepare the Pizza Sauce (if using):**
   - Heat olive oil in a small saucepan over medium heat.
   - Add minced garlic and cook for 1 minute until fragrant.
   - Add tomato sauce, oregano, salt, and black pepper. Simmer for 5 minutes. Remove from heat.

4. **Assemble the Pizza:**
   - Preheat your oven to 475°F (245°C) if using a pizza stone, or 425°F (220°C) for a baking sheet.
   - Roll out the pizza dough on a floured surface to your desired thickness and shape. Transfer to a greased baking sheet or pizza stone.
   - If using, spread a thin layer of pizza sauce over the dough.
   - Evenly distribute the cooked beef and vegetable mixture over the dough.
   - Sprinkle shredded provolone and mozzarella cheese over the top.

5. **Bake the Pizza:**
   - Bake in the preheated oven for 12-15 minutes, or until the crust is golden brown and the cheese is melted and bubbly.

6. **Serve:**
   - Remove the pizza from the oven and let it cool for a few minutes before slicing.
   - Garnish with additional oregano or red pepper flakes if desired.

Enjoy your flavorful Philly Cheesesteak Pizza!

Crab Cakes

Ingredients:

- **Crab Meat:** 1 lb (preferably lump or jumbo lump crab meat, picked over for shells)
- **Mayonnaise:** 1/4 cup
- **Egg:** 1 large
- **Dijon Mustard:** 1 tbsp
- **Worcestershire Sauce:** 1 tsp
- **Old Bay Seasoning:** 1 tsp
- **Parsley:** 2 tbsp, finely chopped
- **Green Onions:** 2, finely chopped
- **Breadcrumbs:** 1/2 cup (preferably panko for extra crunch)
- **Salt:** 1/2 tsp
- **Black Pepper:** 1/4 tsp
- **Olive Oil or Vegetable Oil:** For frying

For Serving (optional):

- **Lemon Wedges:** For garnish
- **Tartar Sauce:** For dipping

Instructions:

1. **Prepare the Crab Mixture:**
   - In a large bowl, gently combine the crab meat, mayonnaise, egg, Dijon mustard, Worcestershire sauce, Old Bay seasoning, chopped parsley, green onions, breadcrumbs, salt, and black pepper.
   - Be careful not to break up the crab meat too much; you want to keep some chunks for texture.
2. **Form the Crab Cakes:**
   - Using your hands or a scoop, form the mixture into patties about 1/2 inch thick. You should get about 6-8 cakes depending on size.
3. **Chill the Crab Cakes:**
   - Place the formed crab cakes on a baking sheet or plate and refrigerate for at least 30 minutes. This helps them hold together better during cooking.
4. **Cook the Crab Cakes:**
   - Heat a large skillet over medium heat and add enough oil to coat the bottom of the pan.
   - Once the oil is hot, carefully add the crab cakes to the skillet. Cook in batches if necessary to avoid overcrowding.
   - Fry the crab cakes for 4-5 minutes per side, or until golden brown and crispy on the outside and heated through.

5. **Drain and Serve:**
    - Transfer the cooked crab cakes to a plate lined with paper towels to drain excess oil.
    - Serve warm with lemon wedges and tartar sauce, if desired.

Enjoy your flavorful and crispy Crab Cakes!

Chicken and Waffles

Ingredients:

For the Chicken:

- **Chicken Pieces:** 4 bone-in, skin-on chicken thighs or breasts (or a mix)
- **Buttermilk:** 2 cups (for marinating)
- **All-Purpose Flour:** 1 cup (for breading)
- **Cornstarch:** 1/4 cup
- **Paprika:** 1 tsp
- **Garlic Powder:** 1 tsp
- **Onion Powder:** 1 tsp
- **Salt:** 1 tsp
- **Black Pepper:** 1/2 tsp
- **Cayenne Pepper:** 1/2 tsp (optional, for heat)
- **Baking Powder:** 1/2 tsp (for extra crispiness)
- **Vegetable Oil:** For frying

For the Waffles:

- **All-Purpose Flour:** 2 cups
- **Baking Powder:** 1 tbsp
- **Sugar:** 2 tbsp
- **Salt:** 1/2 tsp
- **Eggs:** 2 large
- **Milk:** 1 3/4 cups
- **Butter:** 1/2 cup, melted
- **Vanilla Extract:** 1 tsp (optional)

For Serving:

- **Maple Syrup:** For drizzling
- **Butter:** For serving (optional)
- **Powdered Sugar:** For dusting (optional)

Instructions:

1. **Marinate the Chicken:**
   - Place the chicken pieces in a large bowl or zip-top bag and pour in the buttermilk. Cover and refrigerate for at least 2 hours or overnight for the best results.
2. **Prepare the Breading:**
   - In a large bowl, combine flour, cornstarch, paprika, garlic powder, onion powder, salt, black pepper, cayenne pepper, and baking powder.

3. **Bread the Chicken:**
    - Remove the chicken pieces from the buttermilk, letting excess drip off.
    - Dredge each piece in the flour mixture, pressing lightly to adhere. Shake off excess flour and set aside on a rack.
4. **Fry the Chicken:**
    - Heat vegetable oil in a large skillet or deep fryer to 350°F (175°C). You should have enough oil to submerge the chicken pieces halfway.
    - Fry the chicken in batches, if necessary, for about 8-10 minutes per side, or until the chicken is golden brown and the internal temperature reaches 165°F (74°C).
    - Remove the chicken from the oil and place on a paper towel-lined plate to drain.
5. **Prepare the Waffles:**
    - Preheat a waffle iron according to the manufacturer's instructions.
    - In a large bowl, whisk together flour, baking powder, sugar, and salt.
    - In another bowl, whisk together eggs, milk, melted butter, and vanilla extract.
    - Pour the wet ingredients into the dry ingredients and stir until just combined (a few lumps are okay).
    - Lightly grease the waffle iron with non-stick spray or brush with oil.
    - Pour the batter onto the preheated waffle iron and cook according to the manufacturer's instructions, until the waffles are golden brown and crisp.
6. **Assemble and Serve:**
    - Place a waffle on each plate and top with a piece of fried chicken.
    - Drizzle with maple syrup and, if desired, add a pat of butter and a dusting of powdered sugar.

Enjoy your delicious Chicken and Waffles!

Shrimp Po' Boy

Ingredients:

For the Shrimp:

- **Shrimp:** 1 lb, large, peeled and deveined
- **Buttermilk:** 1 cup (for soaking)
- **All-Purpose Flour:** 1 cup
- **Cornmeal:** 1/2 cup
- **Paprika:** 1 tsp
- **Garlic Powder:** 1 tsp
- **Onion Powder:** 1 tsp
- **Cayenne Pepper:** 1/2 tsp (optional, for extra heat)
- **Salt:** 1 tsp
- **Black Pepper:** 1/2 tsp
- **Baking Powder:** 1/2 tsp
- **Vegetable Oil:** For frying

For the Sandwich:

- **French Bread or Po' Boy Rolls:** 4 (split lengthwise)
- **Shredded Lettuce:** 2 cups
- **Tomato:** 1-2, sliced
- **Pickles:** 1/2 cup, sliced
- **Lemon Wedges:** For garnish (optional)

For the Remoulade Sauce:

- **Mayonnaise:** 1/2 cup
- **Creole Mustard:** 2 tbsp (or Dijon mustard)
- **Hot Sauce:** 1 tbsp (adjust to taste)
- **Paprika:** 1/2 tsp
- **Garlic Powder:** 1/2 tsp
- **Cayenne Pepper:** 1/4 tsp (optional)
- **Lemon Juice:** 1 tbsp
- **Chopped Green Onions:** 1 tbsp (optional)
- **Salt:** To taste
- **Black Pepper:** To taste

Instructions:

1. **Prepare the Remoulade Sauce:**

- In a bowl, combine mayonnaise, Creole mustard, hot sauce, paprika, garlic powder, cayenne pepper (if using), lemon juice, and green onions (if using). Season with salt and black pepper to taste. Mix well and refrigerate until ready to use.
2. **Prepare the Shrimp:**
    - Soak the shrimp in buttermilk for about 30 minutes.
    - In a separate bowl, mix together flour, cornmeal, paprika, garlic powder, onion powder, cayenne pepper (if using), salt, black pepper, and baking powder.
3. **Bread the Shrimp:**
    - Remove the shrimp from the buttermilk, allowing excess to drip off.
    - Dredge each shrimp in the flour mixture, pressing lightly to ensure an even coating.
4. **Fry the Shrimp:**
    - Heat vegetable oil in a large skillet or deep fryer to 350°F (175°C).
    - Fry the shrimp in batches, being careful not to overcrowd the pan. Cook for 2-3 minutes per side, or until golden brown and cooked through.
    - Transfer the shrimp to a paper towel-lined plate to drain excess oil.
5. **Assemble the Po' Boys:**
    - Lightly toast or warm the French bread or Po' Boy rolls.
    - Spread a generous amount of remoulade sauce on the inside of each roll.
    - Layer shredded lettuce, tomato slices, pickles, and fried shrimp on the bottom half of each roll.
    - Add more remoulade sauce on top if desired.
6. **Serve:**
    - Garnish with lemon wedges if desired.
    - Serve immediately and enjoy your delicious Shrimp Po' Boy!

This Shrimp Po' Boy combines crispy shrimp with the crunch of fresh vegetables and the tang of remoulade sauce, all nestled in a soft roll for a truly satisfying sandwich.

Sausage and Peppers Sandwich

Ingredients:

For the Sausage:

- **Italian Sausages:** 4 (sweet or hot, depending on your preference)
- **Olive Oil:** 1 tbsp (for grilling or sautéing)

For the Peppers and Onions:

- **Bell Peppers:** 2 (one red, one green), sliced into strips
- **Onion:** 1 large, sliced into rings
- **Olive Oil:** 2 tbsp
- **Garlic:** 2 cloves, minced
- **Salt:** 1/2 tsp
- **Black Pepper:** 1/4 tsp
- **Red Pepper Flakes:** 1/4 tsp (optional, for extra heat)
- **Italian Seasoning:** 1/2 tsp
- **Balsamic Vinegar:** 1 tbsp (optional, for added flavor)

For the Sandwich:

- **Hoagie Rolls or Submarine Rolls:** 4, split lengthwise
- **Provolone Cheese:** 4 slices (optional)
- **Fresh Parsley:** For garnish (optional)

Instructions:

1. **Cook the Sausages:**
   - Preheat a grill or skillet over medium heat. If using a skillet, add 1 tablespoon of olive oil.
   - Cook the sausages, turning occasionally, until they are browned and cooked through (about 12-15 minutes). If grilling, cook over direct heat, turning frequently.
2. **Prepare the Peppers and Onions:**
   - While the sausages are cooking, heat 2 tablespoons of olive oil in a large skillet over medium heat.
   - Add the sliced bell peppers and onions. Cook, stirring occasionally, until the vegetables are softened and slightly caramelized (about 10 minutes).
   - Add the minced garlic, salt, black pepper, red pepper flakes (if using), and Italian seasoning. Cook for an additional 1-2 minutes until fragrant.
   - Stir in the balsamic vinegar if using, and cook for another minute. Remove from heat.

3. **Toast the Rolls:**
    - If desired, lightly toast the hoagie rolls under the broiler or in a toaster oven until they are slightly crispy.
4. **Assemble the Sandwiches:**
    - Place a cooked sausage into each hoagie roll.
    - Top with a generous portion of the sautéed peppers and onions.
    - If using provolone cheese, place a slice on top of the peppers and onions. You can melt the cheese under the broiler for a minute if desired.
5. **Serve:**
    - Garnish with fresh parsley if desired.
    - Serve the sandwiches warm and enjoy!

This Sausage and Peppers Sandwich is a flavorful and satisfying meal, perfect for a casual lunch or dinner.

Jambalaya

Ingredients:

- **Olive Oil:** 2 tbsp
- **Andouille Sausage:** 12 oz, sliced into rounds
- **Chicken Thighs:** 1 lb, boneless and skinless, cut into bite-sized pieces
- **Shrimp:** 1/2 lb, peeled and deveined (optional, can be added at the end)
- **Onion:** 1 large, diced
- **Bell Peppers:** 1 green and 1 red, diced
- **Celery:** 2 stalks, diced
- **Garlic:** 4 cloves, minced
- **Tomatoes:** 1 can (14.5 oz) diced or 2-3 fresh tomatoes, chopped
- **Chicken Broth:** 3 cups
- **Long-Grain Rice:** 1 1/2 cups
- **Bay Leaves:** 2
- **Thyme:** 1 tsp, dried
- **Paprika:** 1 tsp
- **Cayenne Pepper:** 1/2 tsp (adjust to taste)
- **Oregano:** 1/2 tsp
- **Salt:** 1 tsp (or to taste)
- **Black Pepper:** 1/2 tsp
- **Green Onions:** 1/4 cup, chopped (for garnish)
- **Parsley:** 1/4 cup, chopped (for garnish)
- **Hot Sauce:** For serving (optional)

Instructions:

1. **Cook the Sausage:**
   - Heat olive oil in a large pot or Dutch oven over medium heat.
   - Add the sliced andouille sausage and cook until browned, about 5 minutes.
   - Remove the sausage with a slotted spoon and set aside.
2. **Cook the Chicken:**
   - In the same pot, add the chicken pieces. Cook until browned on all sides, about 5-7 minutes.
   - Remove the chicken and set aside with the sausage.
3. **Sauté Vegetables:**
   - Add a little more olive oil if needed.
   - Sauté the diced onion, bell peppers, and celery until softened, about 5 minutes.
   - Add the minced garlic and cook for another 1-2 minutes.
4. **Add Tomatoes and Spices:**
   - Stir in the tomatoes, bay leaves, thyme, paprika, cayenne pepper, oregano, salt, and black pepper.

- Cook for 2-3 minutes, allowing the flavors to combine.
5. **Add Rice and Broth:**
    - Stir in the rice until well-coated with the tomato mixture.
    - Add the chicken broth and bring to a boil.
6. **Simmer:**
    - Reduce the heat to low, cover the pot, and let it simmer for 15-20 minutes, or until the rice is cooked and the liquid is absorbed.
    - Stir occasionally to prevent sticking.
7. **Add Seafood:**
    - If using shrimp, add them during the last 5 minutes of cooking. Stir until the shrimp are pink and cooked through.
8. **Combine and Serve:**
    - Return the sausage and chicken to the pot and stir to combine.
    - Remove the bay leaves.
    - Garnish with chopped green onions and parsley.
    - Serve hot with hot sauce on the side, if desired.

Enjoy your flavorful and comforting Jambalaya, a true taste of Creole cuisine!

Monte Cristo Sandwich

Ingredients:

For the Sandwich:

- **Bread:** 8 slices (white or brioche work best)
- **Deli Ham:** 4 slices
- **Deli Turkey:** 4 slices
- **Swiss Cheese:** 4 slices
- **American Cheese:** 4 slices
- **Dijon Mustard:** 2 tbsp
- **Mayonnaise:** 2 tbsp

For the Egg Batter:

- **Eggs:** 4
- **Milk:** 1/2 cup
- **Salt:** 1/4 tsp
- **Black Pepper:** 1/4 tsp
- **Ground Nutmeg:** 1/4 tsp (optional, for a hint of warmth)
- **Powdered Sugar:** For dusting (optional)

For Frying:

- **Butter:** 4 tbsp (or enough to coat the pan)
- **Vegetable Oil:** 2 tbsp (optional, for extra crispiness)

For Serving:

- **Jelly or Jam:** (such as raspberry or strawberry, for dipping)
- **Lemon Wedges:** For garnish (optional)

Instructions:

1. **Prepare the Sandwiches:**
    - Spread Dijon mustard on one side of 4 slices of bread.
    - Spread mayonnaise on the other side of the same slices.
    - Layer each slice of bread with a slice of Swiss cheese, a slice of American cheese, a slice of ham, and a slice of turkey.
    - Top with another slice of bread to make 4 sandwiches.
2. **Prepare the Egg Batter:**
    - In a shallow dish, whisk together the eggs, milk, salt, pepper, and nutmeg (if using).

3. **Dip the Sandwiches:**
    - Carefully dip each sandwich into the egg batter, ensuring both sides are coated but not soaked. Allow excess to drip off.
4. **Cook the Sandwiches:**
    - Heat a large skillet or griddle over medium heat.
    - Add 1 tablespoon of butter and 1/2 tablespoon of vegetable oil to the skillet. Once melted and hot, add one or two sandwiches (depending on skillet size) to the pan.
    - Cook for 3-4 minutes on each side, or until golden brown and the cheese is melted. You may need to add more butter and oil for additional sandwiches.
5. **Serve:**
    - Remove the sandwiches from the skillet and let them cool slightly.
    - Dust with powdered sugar if desired.
    - Serve with jelly or jam for dipping, and garnish with lemon wedges if desired.

Tips:

- **For a lighter version:** Use fewer slices of cheese or leaner meats.
- **For a crispy texture:** Make sure the skillet is well-buttered and properly heated before adding the sandwiches.

Enjoy your delicious Monte Cristo Sandwich—a perfect blend of savory and sweet!

Greek Salad with Lamb

Ingredients:

For the Lamb:

- **Lamb Chops or Lamb Sirloin:** 1 lb, boneless (cut into bite-sized pieces if using sirloin)
- **Olive Oil:** 2 tbsp
- **Garlic:** 2 cloves, minced
- **Lemon Juice:** 2 tbsp
- **Dried Oregano:** 1 tsp
- **Ground Cumin:** 1/2 tsp
- **Salt:** 1/2 tsp
- **Black Pepper:** 1/4 tsp

For the Greek Salad:

- **Cucumber:** 1 large, peeled and diced
- **Cherry Tomatoes:** 1 cup, halved
- **Red Onion:** 1/2 small, thinly sliced
- **Kalamata Olives:** 1/2 cup, pitted
- **Feta Cheese:** 1/2 cup, crumbled
- **Fresh Parsley:** 2 tbsp, chopped (for garnish)

For the Dressing:

- **Olive Oil:** 1/4 cup
- **Red Wine Vinegar:** 2 tbsp
- **Lemon Juice:** 1 tbsp
- **Dried Oregano:** 1/2 tsp
- **Garlic:** 1 clove, minced
- **Salt:** 1/2 tsp
- **Black Pepper:** 1/4 tsp

Instructions:

1. **Marinate the Lamb:**
    - In a bowl, combine olive oil, minced garlic, lemon juice, dried oregano, ground cumin, salt, and black pepper.
    - Add the lamb chops or pieces and toss to coat well.
    - Marinate for at least 30 minutes (or up to 2 hours) in the refrigerator.
2. **Cook the Lamb:**
    - Heat a grill or skillet over medium-high heat. If using a skillet, add a bit of olive oil to prevent sticking.

- Grill or sear the lamb for 4-5 minutes per side, or until it reaches your desired level of doneness (medium-rare to medium is usually preferred for lamb).
- Remove from heat and let rest for 5 minutes before slicing into bite-sized pieces if needed.

3. **Prepare the Greek Salad:**
   - In a large bowl, combine diced cucumber, cherry tomatoes, sliced red onion, Kalamata olives, and crumbled feta cheese.
   - In a small bowl, whisk together the olive oil, red wine vinegar, lemon juice, dried oregano, minced garlic, salt, and black pepper.
   - Pour the dressing over the salad and toss to coat.
4. **Assemble the Dish:**
   - Place the Greek salad on a serving platter or individual plates.
   - Top with the cooked lamb.
   - Garnish with chopped fresh parsley.
5. **Serve:**
   - Serve immediately, either warm or at room temperature.

Tips:

- **For extra flavor:** Consider adding some roasted red peppers or artichoke hearts to the salad.
- **For a complete meal:** Serve with warm pita bread or over a bed of couscous or quinoa.

This Greek Salad with Lamb is a flavorful and refreshing dish that combines the rich taste of lamb with the crisp, tangy elements of a Greek salad. Enjoy!

BBQ Brisket Sandwich

Ingredients:

For the Brisket:

- **Beef Brisket:** 3-4 lbs, trimmed
- **Olive Oil:** 2 tbsp
- **BBQ Rub:**
    - **Brown Sugar:** 2 tbsp
    - **Paprika:** 2 tbsp
    - **Garlic Powder:** 1 tbsp
    - **Onion Powder:** 1 tbsp
    - **Ground Cumin:** 1 tsp
    - **Chili Powder:** 1 tsp
    - **Salt:** 1 tbsp
    - **Black Pepper:** 1 tsp
    - **Cayenne Pepper:** 1/2 tsp (optional, for heat)

For the BBQ Sauce:

- **Ketchup:** 1 cup
- **Apple Cider Vinegar:** 1/4 cup
- **Brown Sugar:** 1/4 cup
- **Honey:** 2 tbsp
- **Worcestershire Sauce:** 2 tbsp
- **Smoked Paprika:** 1 tsp
- **Garlic Powder:** 1/2 tsp
- **Onion Powder:** 1/2 tsp
- **Salt:** 1/2 tsp
- **Black Pepper:** 1/4 tsp
- **Hot Sauce:** To taste (optional)

For the Sandwich:

- **Hamburger Buns or Sandwich Rolls:** 4-6, lightly toasted
- **Coleslaw:** 2 cups (optional, for topping)
- **Pickles:** For garnish (optional)

Instructions:

1. **Prepare the Brisket:**
    - Preheat your oven to 300°F (150°C).
    - Mix all the BBQ rub ingredients together in a small bowl.

- Rub the brisket all over with olive oil, then apply the BBQ rub generously, coating all sides.
- Place the brisket in a roasting pan or on a rack set inside a baking dish. Cover tightly with aluminum foil.

2. **Cook the Brisket:**
   - Roast in the preheated oven for about 3-4 hours, or until the brisket is tender and easily shreds with a fork. Cooking time can vary based on the size of the brisket.
   - Once done, remove from the oven and let rest for 15-20 minutes before slicing or shredding.

3. **Prepare the BBQ Sauce:**
   - While the brisket is cooking, combine all the BBQ sauce ingredients in a saucepan.
   - Simmer over low heat for about 10-15 minutes, stirring occasionally, until the sauce is slightly thickened. Adjust seasoning with salt, pepper, and hot sauce as needed.

4. **Assemble the Sandwiches:**
   - Shred or slice the cooked brisket.
   - Warm the BBQ sauce and toss the shredded brisket in the sauce until well-coated.
   - Place a generous amount of BBQ brisket on the bottom half of each toasted bun or roll.
   - Top with coleslaw and pickles if desired.
   - Cover with the top half of the bun.

5. **Serve:**
   - Serve the BBQ brisket sandwiches hot and enjoy!

Tips:

- **For extra tenderness:** Let the brisket rest in the cooking juices for a few minutes before slicing or shredding.
- **For a smoky flavor:** Add a bit of smoked paprika or liquid smoke to the BBQ sauce.

This BBQ Brisket Sandwich is perfect for a hearty meal, combining tender brisket with tangy BBQ sauce and crunchy coleslaw. Enjoy!

Turkey Chili

Ingredients:

For the Chili:

- **Ground Turkey:** 1 lb
- **Olive Oil:** 2 tbsp
- **Onion:** 1 large, diced
- **Bell Pepper:** 1 red or green, diced
- **Garlic:** 3 cloves, minced
- **Carrot:** 1 large, peeled and diced
- **Celery:** 2 stalks, diced
- **Tomatoes:** 1 can (14.5 oz) diced tomatoes
- **Tomato Paste:** 2 tbsp
- **Chicken Broth:** 2 cups
- **Kidney Beans:** 1 can (15 oz), drained and rinsed
- **Black Beans:** 1 can (15 oz), drained and rinsed
- **Corn:** 1 cup, frozen or fresh
- **Chili Powder:** 2 tbsp
- **Ground Cumin:** 1 tsp
- **Paprika:** 1 tsp
- **Oregano:** 1 tsp
- **Salt:** 1 tsp (or to taste)
- **Black Pepper:** 1/2 tsp
- **Red Pepper Flakes:** 1/4 tsp (optional, for heat)
- **Bay Leaf:** 1

For Garnish (Optional):

- **Chopped Fresh Cilantro**
- **Shredded Cheddar Cheese**
- **Sour Cream**
- **Sliced Jalapeños**
- **Diced Avocado**

Instructions:

1. **Cook the Turkey:**
   - Heat olive oil in a large pot or Dutch oven over medium heat.
   - Add the ground turkey and cook until browned, breaking it up with a spoon as it cooks. Drain any excess fat.
2. **Sauté Vegetables:**

- - Add the diced onion, bell pepper, carrot, and celery to the pot. Cook until the vegetables are softened, about 5-7 minutes.
  - Stir in the minced garlic and cook for another 1-2 minutes, until fragrant.
3. **Add Tomato and Spices:**
   - Stir in the tomato paste and cook for 2 minutes.
   - Add the diced tomatoes (with their juice), chicken broth, kidney beans, black beans, corn, chili powder, ground cumin, paprika, oregano, salt, black pepper, red pepper flakes (if using), and bay leaf.
4. **Simmer:**
   - Bring the mixture to a boil, then reduce heat to low and let simmer, uncovered, for about 30 minutes. Stir occasionally. The chili should thicken slightly and the flavors should meld together.
5. **Adjust Seasoning:**
   - Taste and adjust seasoning if necessary. Remove the bay leaf before serving.
6. **Serve:**
   - Ladle the chili into bowls.
   - Garnish with chopped fresh cilantro, shredded cheddar cheese, a dollop of sour cream, sliced jalapeños, or diced avocado if desired.

Tips:

- **For a thicker chili:** Simmer longer to reduce the liquid, or mash some of the beans with a fork to thicken the texture.
- **For added depth:** Consider adding a splash of lime juice or a bit of cocoa powder to enhance the flavor.

This Turkey Chili is perfect for a cozy meal and can be easily customized with your favorite toppings. Enjoy!

Breakfast Burrito

Ingredients:

For the Filling:

- **Bacon:** 4 slices, cooked until crispy and crumbled (or use breakfast sausage or ham if preferred)
- **Potatoes:** 1 medium, peeled and diced (or use frozen hash browns)
- **Olive Oil:** 1-2 tbsp (for cooking potatoes)
- **Eggs:** 4
- **Milk:** 1/4 cup
- **Salt:** 1/2 tsp
- **Black Pepper:** 1/4 tsp
- **Cheddar Cheese:** 1/2 cup, shredded (or use your favorite cheese)
- **Green Onions:** 2 tbsp, chopped (optional)
- **Bell Pepper:** 1/2, diced (optional)
- **Spinach:** 1 cup, chopped (optional)

For the Burrito:

- **Flour Tortillas:** 4 large (10-inch size works well)
- **Salsa:** For serving (optional)
- **Sour Cream:** For serving (optional)
- **Avocado:** Sliced (optional)
- **Hot Sauce:** For serving (optional)

Instructions:

1. **Cook the Potatoes:**
   - Heat olive oil in a large skillet over medium heat.
   - Add the diced potatoes and cook, stirring occasionally, until they are crispy and golden brown, about 10-15 minutes. Season with salt and pepper. Remove from the skillet and set aside.
2. **Scramble the Eggs:**
   - In a bowl, whisk together the eggs, milk, salt, and black pepper.
   - In the same skillet used for the potatoes (wipe out excess oil if necessary), pour in the egg mixture. Cook over medium heat, stirring gently until the eggs are scrambled and cooked through. Remove from heat.
3. **Combine Ingredients:**
   - Add the cooked bacon, shredded cheese, and any optional ingredients like green onions, bell pepper, or spinach to the scrambled eggs. Stir to combine and let the cheese melt slightly.
4. **Assemble the Burritos:**

- Warm the flour tortillas in a dry skillet or microwave for easier rolling.
- Lay out each tortilla and evenly distribute the potato mixture in the center of each tortilla.
- Top with the egg and cheese mixture.
- Fold in the sides of the tortilla and roll up from the bottom to form a burrito.

5. **Optional: Toast the Burritos:**
   - For a crispy exterior, heat a clean skillet over medium heat. Place the burrito seam side down and cook until golden brown and crispy, about 2 minutes per side.
6. **Serve:**
   - Cut the burritos in half if desired.
   - Serve with salsa, sour cream, sliced avocado, or hot sauce.

Tips:

- **For extra flavor:** Add some sautéed onions, mushrooms, or your favorite veggies to the filling.
- **Make ahead:** Prepare the filling in advance and refrigerate. Reheat the filling and assemble the burritos in the morning for a quick breakfast.

Enjoy your delicious Breakfast Burrito—perfect for starting your day off right!

Cajun Chicken Pasta

Ingredients:

For the Chicken:

- **Chicken Breasts:** 2 large, boneless and skinless
- **Olive Oil:** 2 tbsp
- **Cajun Seasoning:** 2 tbsp (store-bought or homemade, see note below)
- **Salt:** 1/2 tsp
- **Black Pepper:** 1/4 tsp

For the Pasta and Sauce:

- **Pasta:** 8 oz (penne, fettuccine, or your choice)
- **Butter:** 2 tbsp
- **Garlic:** 3 cloves, minced
- **Onion:** 1 small, diced
- **Red Bell Pepper:** 1, sliced
- **Green Bell Pepper:** 1, sliced
- **Heavy Cream:** 1 cup
- **Chicken Broth:** 1/2 cup
- **Parmesan Cheese:** 1/2 cup, grated
- **Dried Thyme:** 1/2 tsp
- **Paprika:** 1/2 tsp
- **Cajun Seasoning:** 1 tsp (optional, adjust to taste)
- **Salt:** To taste
- **Black Pepper:** To taste
- **Fresh Parsley:** 2 tbsp, chopped (for garnish)

Instructions:

1. **Cook the Pasta:**
    - Bring a large pot of salted water to a boil. Cook the pasta according to the package instructions until al dente.
    - Drain and set aside.
2. **Prepare the Chicken:**
    - Rub the chicken breasts with olive oil, Cajun seasoning, salt, and black pepper.
    - Heat a large skillet over medium-high heat. Add a little more olive oil if needed.
    - Cook the chicken breasts for 6-7 minutes per side, or until fully cooked and the internal temperature reaches 165°F (75°C). Remove from the skillet and let rest for 5 minutes before slicing into strips.
3. **Make the Sauce:**
    - In the same skillet, add 2 tablespoons of butter and melt over medium heat.

- Add the diced onion and cook until translucent, about 3-4 minutes.
- Add the minced garlic and cook for another minute until fragrant.
- Stir in the sliced red and green bell peppers and cook until tender, about 4 minutes.
- Pour in the heavy cream and chicken broth, and bring to a simmer.
- Stir in the grated Parmesan cheese, dried thyme, paprika, and additional Cajun seasoning if desired. Continue to simmer until the sauce is slightly thickened, about 3-5 minutes. Adjust seasoning with salt and black pepper to taste.

4. **Combine Pasta and Sauce:**
   - Add the cooked pasta to the sauce and toss to coat.
   - Add the sliced chicken on top and gently mix everything together.
5. **Serve:**
   - Garnish with chopped fresh parsley.
   - Serve immediately, and enjoy!

Homemade Cajun Seasoning (Optional):

If you prefer homemade Cajun seasoning, you can mix the following spices:

- **Paprika:** 2 tbsp
- **Onion Powder:** 1 tbsp
- **Garlic Powder:** 1 tbsp
- **Oregano:** 1 tsp
- **Thyme:** 1 tsp
- **Cayenne Pepper:** 1/2 tsp (adjust to taste)
- **Salt:** 1 tsp
- **Black Pepper:** 1/2 tsp

Tips:

- **For extra heat:** Add a pinch of red pepper flakes to the sauce.
- **For a healthier version:** Use half-and-half instead of heavy cream, or substitute with a dairy-free cream.

This Cajun Chicken Pasta combines the bold flavors of Cajun seasoning with a creamy, cheesy sauce for a comforting and satisfying dish. Enjoy!

Grilled Veggie Panini

Ingredients:

For the Vegetables:

- **Zucchini:** 1 medium, sliced
- **Red Bell Pepper:** 1, sliced
- **Yellow Bell Pepper:** 1, sliced
- **Red Onion:** 1 small, sliced
- **Eggplant:** 1 small, sliced (optional)
- **Olive Oil:** 2-3 tbsp
- **Salt:** 1/2 tsp
- **Black Pepper:** 1/4 tsp
- **Balsamic Vinegar:** 1 tbsp (optional, for added flavor)

For the Panini:

- **Ciabatta Bread:** 4 large rolls or 2 ciabatta loaves, halved
- **Hummus:** 1/2 cup (flavor of your choice, such as classic or roasted red pepper)
- **Provolone Cheese:** 4 slices (or mozzarella, fontina, or your favorite cheese)
- **Fresh Basil Leaves:** 8-10
- **Baby Spinach:** 1 cup (optional)
- **Pesto:** 1/4 cup (optional, for extra flavor)

Instructions:

1. **Grill the Vegetables:**
   - Preheat a grill or grill pan over medium-high heat.
   - Toss the sliced vegetables with olive oil, salt, and black pepper.
   - Grill the vegetables in batches, if necessary, until they are tender and have nice grill marks, about 4-5 minutes per side. Optionally, drizzle with balsamic vinegar just before removing from the grill.
2. **Prepare the Panini:**
   - Preheat a panini press or a regular skillet over medium heat. If using a skillet, you may need to press down on the sandwiches with a heavy pan or a spatula.
   - Spread hummus evenly on the cut sides of each ciabatta roll.
   - Layer the grilled vegetables on the bottom half of each roll.
   - Top with a slice of provolone cheese, fresh basil leaves, and baby spinach if using.
   - If desired, spread pesto on the top half of the rolls before closing the sandwiches.
3. **Grill the Panini:**
   - Place the assembled sandwiches in the preheated panini press or skillet.

- Grill for about 3-4 minutes, or until the bread is crispy and the cheese is melted. If using a skillet, flip the sandwiches carefully halfway through the grilling process.
4. **Serve:**
    - Remove from the panini press or skillet.
    - Cut the panini in half if desired and serve immediately.

Tips:

- **For extra flavor:** Add some sun-dried tomatoes or roasted red peppers to the sandwich.
- **For a different cheese:** Goat cheese or feta can add a tangy twist.
- **To make it vegan:** Use vegan cheese and hummus.

This Grilled Veggie Panini is a great way to enjoy a variety of vegetables with the comforting, crispy goodness of a pressed sandwich. Enjoy your delicious and hearty meal!

Pulled Pork Tacos

Ingredients:

For the Pulled Pork:

- **Pork Shoulder (or Pork Butt):** 3-4 lbs, trimmed
- **Olive Oil:** 2 tbsp
- **Onion:** 1 large, chopped
- **Garlic:** 4 cloves, minced
- **Chicken Broth:** 1 cup
- **BBQ Sauce:** 1/2 cup (your favorite or homemade)
- **Apple Cider Vinegar:** 1/4 cup
- **Brown Sugar:** 2 tbsp
- **Paprika:** 1 tbsp
- **Ground Cumin:** 1 tsp
- **Chili Powder:** 1 tsp
- **Ground Black Pepper:** 1/2 tsp
- **Salt:** 1 tsp
- **Red Pepper Flakes:** 1/4 tsp (optional, for heat)
- **Bay Leaf:** 1 (optional)

For the Tacos:

- **Corn or Flour Tortillas:** 8-10
- **Cabbage Slaw:** 2 cups (pre-made or homemade, recipe below)
- **Fresh Cilantro:** 1/4 cup, chopped
- **Lime Wedges:** For serving
- **Avocado:** Sliced (optional)
- **Sour Cream:** For serving (optional)
- **Salsa or Pico de Gallo:** For serving (optional)

For the Cabbage Slaw (optional but recommended):

- **Shredded Cabbage:** 2 cups (green or a mix of green and red)
- **Carrot:** 1, grated
- **Red Onion:** 1/4, thinly sliced
- **Cilantro:** 1/4 cup, chopped
- **Lime Juice:** 2 tbsp
- **Olive Oil:** 1 tbsp
- **Honey:** 1 tsp
- **Salt:** 1/4 tsp
- **Black Pepper:** 1/4 tsp

Instructions:

1. **Prepare the Pulled Pork:**
    - **Sear the Pork:** Heat olive oil in a large skillet or Dutch oven over medium-high heat. Season the pork shoulder with salt and pepper. Sear the pork on all sides until browned, about 3-4 minutes per side. Remove from the skillet and set aside.
    - **Cook the Pork:** In the same skillet, add chopped onion and cook until softened, about 5 minutes. Add minced garlic and cook for another minute. Pour in the chicken broth, apple cider vinegar, BBQ sauce, and stir in the brown sugar, paprika, cumin, chili powder, black pepper, and red pepper flakes if using.
    - **Slow Cook:** Return the pork to the skillet, cover, and cook on low heat for 3-4 hours, or until the pork is tender and easily shreds with a fork. Alternatively, you can use a slow cooker on low for 6-8 hours.
    - **Shred the Pork:** Remove the pork from the skillet and shred with two forks. Return the shredded pork to the sauce and stir to combine. Adjust seasoning if needed.
2. **Prepare the Cabbage Slaw (if using):**
    - In a large bowl, combine shredded cabbage, grated carrot, red onion, and cilantro.
    - In a small bowl, whisk together lime juice, olive oil, honey, salt, and black pepper.
    - Pour the dressing over the cabbage mixture and toss to coat. Let it sit for at least 15 minutes to allow flavors to meld.
3. **Warm the Tortillas:**
    - Heat the tortillas in a dry skillet over medium heat until warm and pliable. Alternatively, warm them in the oven or microwave.
4. **Assemble the Tacos:**
    - Spoon the pulled pork onto each tortilla.
    - Top with cabbage slaw, fresh cilantro, and avocado slices if desired.
    - Serve with lime wedges, sour cream, and salsa or pico de gallo on the side.

Tips:

- **For extra flavor:** Add pickled jalapeños or sliced radishes to the tacos.
- **For a smoky taste:** Incorporate a bit of smoked paprika or liquid smoke into the pulled pork.

These Pulled Pork Tacos are packed with flavor and topped with fresh ingredients, making them perfect for a casual meal or entertaining guests. Enjoy!

Steak Frites

Ingredients:

For the Steak:

- **Ribeye Steak:** 2 (about 1-inch thick, 8-10 oz each) or your preferred cut (e.g., sirloin, flank)
- **Olive Oil:** 2 tbsp
- **Garlic:** 2 cloves, minced
- **Fresh Thyme:** 1 tsp, chopped (or 1/2 tsp dried thyme)
- **Salt:** 1 tsp
- **Black Pepper:** 1/2 tsp

For the Frites:

- **Russet Potatoes:** 2 large, peeled
- **Vegetable Oil:** For frying (enough to fill the pot about 2 inches)
- **Salt:** To taste

For the Sauce (Optional):

- **Beef Stock:** 1/2 cup
- **Red Wine:** 1/4 cup (optional)
- **Shallot:** 1, finely chopped
- **Butter:** 2 tbsp
- **Fresh Thyme:** 1 tsp
- **Salt and Black Pepper:** To taste

Instructions:

1. **Prepare the Frites:**
    - **Cut the Potatoes:** Cut the peeled potatoes into thin matchsticks or wedges.
    - **Soak:** Place the cut potatoes in a bowl of cold water and let soak for at least 30 minutes to remove excess starch. This helps them become crispy when fried.
    - **Dry:** Drain and pat the potatoes dry with paper towels.
2. **Fry the Frites:**
    - **Heat the Oil:** In a deep pot or large skillet, heat vegetable oil to 350°F (175°C). Use a thermometer to ensure the correct temperature.
    - **Fry:** Carefully add the potatoes in batches to avoid overcrowding. Fry until golden brown and crispy, about 4-5 minutes per batch. Remove with a slotted spoon and drain on paper towels. Season with salt immediately while still hot.
3. **Prepare the Steak:**

- **Season the Steak:** Rub the steaks with olive oil, minced garlic, chopped thyme, salt, and black pepper.
- **Cook the Steak:** Heat a large skillet or grill pan over medium-high heat. Add the steaks and cook to your desired doneness (about 4-5 minutes per side for medium-rare, depending on thickness). Adjust cooking time for your preferred doneness. Let the steaks rest for 5 minutes before slicing.

4. **Make the Sauce (Optional):**
   - **Sauté Shallots:** In the same skillet used for the steak (remove excess fat if necessary), add a little butter and sauté the shallots until softened, about 2-3 minutes.
   - **Deglaze the Pan:** Add the beef stock and red wine (if using), scraping up any browned bits from the bottom of the pan. Simmer until the liquid reduces by half, about 5-7 minutes.
   - **Finish the Sauce:** Stir in the remaining butter and fresh thyme. Season with salt and black pepper to taste.
5. **Serve:**
   - **Plate the Dish:** Slice the rested steak and serve with a generous portion of frites.
   - **Add Sauce:** Drizzle the optional sauce over the steak or serve on the side.

Tips:

- **For extra flavor:** You can add a dollop of herb butter or compound butter to the steak just before serving.
- **For crispy frites:** Make sure the oil is hot enough and avoid overcrowding the pot.

Steak Frites is a classic dish that brings together a perfectly cooked steak and crispy, golden fries for a truly satisfying meal. Enjoy!

Chicken Parmesan Sandwich

Ingredients:

For the Chicken:

- **Chicken Breasts:** 2 large, boneless and skinless
- **Flour:** 1/2 cup
- **Eggs:** 2, beaten
- **Breadcrumbs:** 1 cup (preferably Italian-seasoned)
- **Parmesan Cheese:** 1/2 cup, grated
- **Salt:** 1/2 tsp
- **Black Pepper:** 1/4 tsp
- **Garlic Powder:** 1/2 tsp
- **Olive Oil:** For frying

For Assembly:

- **Marinara Sauce:** 1 cup (store-bought or homemade)
- **Mozzarella Cheese:** 4 slices or 1 cup shredded
- **Fresh Basil:** 4-6 leaves, optional for garnish
- **Crusty Rolls or Sub Buns:** 4 (hoagie rolls or Italian bread works well)
- **Salt and Pepper:** To taste

Instructions:

1. **Prepare the Chicken:**
    - **Flatten the Chicken:** Place the chicken breasts between two pieces of plastic wrap or parchment paper. Gently pound them with a meat mallet or rolling pin until they are an even thickness (about 1/2 inch).
    - **Season and Bread:** Set up a breading station: Place flour in one bowl, beaten eggs in another, and a mixture of breadcrumbs, grated Parmesan, salt, black pepper, and garlic powder in a third bowl.
    - **Coat the Chicken:** Dredge each chicken breast in flour, shaking off the excess. Dip in the beaten eggs, then coat thoroughly with the breadcrumb mixture.
2. **Cook the Chicken:**
    - **Heat Oil:** In a large skillet, heat olive oil over medium heat. You need enough oil to cover the bottom of the pan.
    - **Fry the Chicken:** Fry the breaded chicken breasts for about 4-5 minutes per side, or until golden brown and cooked through (internal temperature should reach 165°F or 75°C). Remove from the skillet and drain on paper towels.
3. **Assemble the Sandwiches:**
    - **Preheat Oven (Optional):** Preheat the oven to 375°F (190°C) if you want to melt the cheese in the oven.

- **Prepare Rolls:** Split the rolls or sub buns and lightly toast them if desired.
- **Add Sauce and Cheese:** Place the cooked chicken breasts on the bottom half of each roll. Spoon marinara sauce over each piece of chicken, then top with mozzarella cheese.
- **Melt Cheese (Optional):** Place the sandwiches on a baking sheet and bake in the preheated oven for about 5 minutes, or until the cheese is melted and bubbly.

4. **Serve:**
   - **Garnish:** Top with fresh basil leaves if desired.
   - **Finish:** Season with salt and pepper to taste.
   - **Close and Serve:** Close the sandwiches with the top half of the roll and serve hot.

Tips:

- **For extra flavor:** Add a sprinkle of dried oregano or Italian seasoning to the breadcrumb mixture.
- **For a spicier kick:** Add a few red pepper flakes to the marinara sauce.

This Chicken Parmesan Sandwich combines crispy, breaded chicken with gooey cheese and savory marinara sauce, all packed into a delicious roll. It's a comforting and satisfying meal that's always a hit!

Beef Stroganoff

Ingredients:

For the Beef:

- **Beef Sirloin or Tenderloin:** 1 lb, cut into thin strips (or use beef stew meat for a budget-friendly option)
- **Olive Oil:** 2 tbsp
- **Butter:** 2 tbsp
- **Salt:** 1 tsp
- **Black Pepper:** 1/2 tsp
- **Paprika:** 1 tsp

For the Sauce:

- **Onion:** 1 medium, finely chopped
- **Garlic:** 2 cloves, minced
- **Mushrooms:** 8 oz, sliced (cremini, button, or a mix)
- **Beef Broth:** 1 cup
- **Worcestershire Sauce:** 1 tbsp
- **Dijon Mustard:** 1 tbsp
- **Flour:** 1 tbsp (for thickening)
- **Sour Cream:** 1/2 cup
- **Heavy Cream:** 1/4 cup (optional, for extra creaminess)
- **Fresh Parsley:** 2 tbsp, chopped (for garnish)

For Serving:

- **Egg Noodles, Rice, or Mashed Potatoes:** Cooked, for serving

Instructions:

1. **Prepare the Beef:**
   - **Season:** Season the beef strips with salt, black pepper, and paprika.
   - **Sear:** Heat olive oil and 1 tablespoon of butter in a large skillet or sauté pan over medium-high heat. Add the beef in batches to avoid overcrowding. Sear the beef for 2-3 minutes on each side, or until browned. Remove from the skillet and set aside.
2. **Make the Sauce:**
   - **Sauté Vegetables:** In the same skillet, add the remaining 1 tablespoon of butter. Sauté the chopped onion until softened, about 3-4 minutes. Add the minced garlic and cook for another minute.

- **Cook Mushrooms:** Add the sliced mushrooms and cook until they are browned and tender, about 5-6 minutes.
- **Deglaze:** Stir in the flour and cook for 1-2 minutes, allowing it to lightly brown.
- **Add Liquids:** Pour in the beef broth, Worcestershire sauce, and Dijon mustard. Stir well, scraping up any browned bits from the bottom of the pan.
- **Simmer:** Bring the mixture to a simmer and cook for 5 minutes, or until the sauce starts to thicken.

3. **Combine Beef and Sauce:**
   - **Return Beef:** Return the seared beef along with any juices to the skillet. Stir to combine and cook for an additional 5 minutes, or until the beef is heated through and the sauce has thickened to your liking.
   - **Add Cream:** Reduce heat to low and stir in the sour cream and heavy cream (if using). Cook gently for 2-3 minutes, or until the sauce is creamy and heated through. Do not let it boil.
4. **Serve:**
   - **Garnish:** Sprinkle with fresh chopped parsley.
   - **Serve:** Serve the Beef Stroganoff over cooked egg noodles, rice, or mashed potatoes.

Tips:

- **For a richer flavor:** Use a combination of beef broth and red wine or sherry.
- **For a thicker sauce:** You can add more flour or a cornstarch slurry (1 tbsp cornstarch mixed with 1 tbsp water) if needed.
- **For added depth:** Include a splash of brandy or a pinch of nutmeg in the sauce.

Beef Stroganoff is a comforting classic that's both creamy and hearty, perfect for a cozy meal. Enjoy this savory dish with your favorite side!

Sweet Potato Fries

Ingredients:

- **Sweet Potatoes:** 2 large, peeled
- **Olive Oil:** 2-3 tbsp
- **Salt:** 1/2 tsp
- **Black Pepper:** 1/4 tsp
- **Paprika:** 1/2 tsp
- **Garlic Powder:** 1/2 tsp
- **Onion Powder:** 1/2 tsp
- **Cayenne Pepper:** 1/4 tsp (optional, for heat)
- **Fresh or Dried Rosemary:** 1 tsp, chopped (optional, for extra flavor)

Instructions:

1. **Preheat Oven:**
   - Preheat your oven to 425°F (220°C). Line a baking sheet with parchment paper or lightly grease it.
2. **Prepare Sweet Potatoes:**
   - **Cut:** Peel the sweet potatoes and cut them into thin strips or wedges, about 1/4 to 1/2 inch thick. Try to keep the pieces as uniform as possible for even cooking.
   - **Soak (Optional):** For extra crispiness, soak the sweet potato strips in cold water for at least 30 minutes. This helps remove excess starch. Drain and pat them dry thoroughly with paper towels.
3. **Season and Toss:**
   - In a large bowl, toss the sweet potato strips with olive oil, salt, black pepper, paprika, garlic powder, onion powder, cayenne pepper (if using), and rosemary (if using). Make sure all the pieces are evenly coated.
4. **Bake:**
   - **Arrange:** Spread the sweet potato strips in a single layer on the prepared baking sheet. Avoid overcrowding to ensure they cook evenly and become crispy.
   - **Bake:** Bake in the preheated oven for 20-25 minutes, flipping the fries halfway through, until they are golden brown and crispy on the edges. Keep an eye on them towards the end to avoid burning.
5. **Serve:**
   - Remove from the oven and let cool for a few minutes. Season with a little extra salt if needed.
   - Serve hot with your favorite dipping sauces, such as ketchup, aioli, or a spicy sriracha mayo.

Tips:

- **For extra crispiness:** You can also add a tablespoon of cornstarch to the seasoning mix before tossing the sweet potatoes.
- **For a different flavor:** Experiment with other seasonings like cumin, chili powder, or cinnamon for a unique twist.
- **For a more even cook:** Consider using a convection oven if you have one, as it helps to crisp the fries more evenly.

These Sweet Potato Fries are a healthier alternative to traditional fries and pack a sweet, savory punch. They make a great accompaniment to burgers, sandwiches, or as a tasty snack on their own. Enjoy!

Loaded Potato Skins

Ingredients:

- **Russet Potatoes:** 4 large
- **Olive Oil:** 2 tbsp
- **Salt:** 1/2 tsp
- **Black Pepper:** 1/4 tsp
- **Cheddar Cheese:** 1 cup, shredded
- **Cooked Bacon:** 6 strips, crumbled
- **Green Onions:** 2-3, chopped (for garnish)
- **Sour Cream:** 1/2 cup (for serving)
- **Chives:** Optional, for garnish

Instructions:

1. **Prepare the Potatoes:**
   - **Preheat Oven:** Preheat your oven to 400°F (200°C).
   - **Bake Potatoes:** Scrub the potatoes and prick them a few times with a fork. Place them directly on the oven rack and bake for about 45-60 minutes, or until tender. Allow them to cool enough to handle.
2. **Prepare the Potato Skins:**
   - **Cut and Scoop:** Once the potatoes are cool, cut them in half lengthwise. Scoop out the flesh, leaving about 1/4 inch of potato on the skin. Save the scooped-out potato flesh for another use (like mashed potatoes or potato soup).
   - **Brush with Oil:** Brush the inside and outside of the potato skins with olive oil and season with salt and pepper.
3. **Crisp the Skins:**
   - **Bake Again:** Place the potato skins cut-side down on a baking sheet. Bake in the preheated oven for 10-15 minutes, or until the skins are crisp and golden brown. Flip the skins over halfway through baking.
4. **Add Toppings:**
   - **Cheese and Bacon:** Remove the potato skins from the oven. Sprinkle shredded cheddar cheese evenly over each skin and top with crumbled bacon.
   - **Return to Oven:** Bake for an additional 5-7 minutes, or until the cheese is melted and bubbly.
5. **Garnish and Serve:**
   - **Garnish:** Remove from the oven and sprinkle with chopped green onions and optional chives.
   - **Serve:** Serve hot with a dollop of sour cream on the side.

Tips:

- **For extra flavor:** Add a sprinkle of paprika or garlic powder to the potato skins before baking.
- **To make it a meal:** Top the loaded potato skins with additional toppings like chili or pulled pork for a hearty twist.
- **For a healthier version:** Use a small amount of cheese and bacon, and consider using Greek yogurt instead of sour cream.

Loaded Potato Skins are crispy, cheesy, and packed with flavor, making them a fantastic choice for game day, parties, or as a fun treat. Enjoy every bite!

Teriyaki Chicken Bowl

Ingredients:

For the Teriyaki Chicken:

- **Chicken Thighs or Breasts:** 1 lb, boneless and skinless (thighs preferred for juiciness)
- **Soy Sauce:** 1/4 cup
- **Mirin:** 1/4 cup (or white wine or dry sherry as a substitute)
- **Brown Sugar:** 2 tbsp
- **Rice Vinegar:** 1 tbsp
- **Garlic:** 2 cloves, minced
- **Ginger:** 1 tsp, grated
- **Cornstarch:** 1 tbsp (for thickening, optional)
- **Water:** 2 tbsp (for cornstarch slurry)
- **Sesame Oil:** 1 tbsp
- **Vegetable Oil:** 1 tbsp (for cooking)

For the Bowl:

- **Rice:** 2 cups cooked (white rice, jasmine rice, or brown rice)
- **Broccoli:** 1 cup, cut into florets
- **Carrots:** 1 large, julienned or sliced
- **Bell Pepper:** 1, sliced (red or yellow)
- **Snow Peas:** 1/2 cup (optional)
- **Green Onions:** 2, chopped (for garnish)
- **Sesame Seeds:** 1 tbsp (for garnish, optional)
- **Fresh Cilantro:** A few sprigs (optional, for garnish)

Instructions:

1. **Prepare the Teriyaki Sauce:**
    - **Mix Ingredients:** In a small saucepan, combine soy sauce, mirin, brown sugar, rice vinegar, minced garlic, and grated ginger. Bring to a simmer over medium heat, stirring occasionally.
    - **Thicken Sauce (Optional):** If you prefer a thicker sauce, mix cornstarch and water in a small bowl to create a slurry. Stir the slurry into the sauce and cook for an additional 1-2 minutes until thickened. Remove from heat.
2. **Cook the Chicken:**
    - **Prepare Chicken:** Season the chicken thighs or breasts with a little salt and pepper.
    - **Sear Chicken:** Heat vegetable oil in a large skillet or pan over medium-high heat. Add the chicken and cook for 5-7 minutes per side, or until cooked through

(internal temperature should reach 165°F or 75°C). Remove from the pan and let rest for a few minutes.
  - **Glaze Chicken:** Slice the cooked chicken and return it to the skillet. Pour the teriyaki sauce over the chicken and cook for an additional 2-3 minutes, allowing the chicken to absorb the sauce.
3. **Prepare the Vegetables:**
   - **Steam or Sauté:** Steam or sauté the broccoli, carrots, bell pepper, and snow peas until tender-crisp. You can do this in a separate pan or in the microwave if you prefer.
4. **Assemble the Bowl:**
   - **Rice Base:** Place a serving of cooked rice in each bowl.
   - **Add Toppings:** Arrange the cooked vegetables and sliced teriyaki chicken on top of the rice.
   - **Garnish:** Sprinkle with chopped green onions, sesame seeds, and fresh cilantro if desired.
5. **Serve:**
   - **Enjoy:** Serve immediately while everything is warm.

Tips:

- **For added flavor:** Marinate the chicken in a portion of the teriyaki sauce for 30 minutes before cooking.
- **For a crunchy texture:** Add some sliced radishes or shredded cabbage as a topping.
- **For spice:** Incorporate a drizzle of sriracha or a sprinkle of red pepper flakes if you like a bit of heat.

This Teriyaki Chicken Bowl is a complete and delicious meal that combines savory, sweet, and fresh elements into one satisfying dish. Enjoy!

www.ingramcontent.com/pod-product-compliance
Lightning Source LLC
LaVergne TN
LVHW081607060526
838201LV00054B/2116